CONSERVATION FRAMING

BY

VIVIAN C. KISTLER, CPF, GCF

ACKNOWLEDGEMENTS

Special thanks to the following framers
and organizations for providing information
and encouraging development of
education in the picture framing industry.

American Paper Institute
Art Business News
Art World News
Book & Paper Group of American Institute for
Conservation of Historic & Artistic Works
James Byrd
Jared Bark, CPF
Carolyn Birchenall CPF
Roy Carter, CPF
Kaye Evans, CPF
Fine Art Trade Guild
Crescent Cardboard Company
Decor Magazine
Paul Frederick, CPF
The Professional Picture Framers Association
Jeff Wanee CPF
Jeffrey L. Neumann
Oberlin College
Dr. Richard Smith
Shan Linde, CPF
Picture Framing Magazine
Paul MacFarland CPF
William P. Parker, CPF
Don Pierce
Roy Rowlands, CPF
Brian Wolf, CPF, GCF
Joyce Zabell, CPF

•

Robert Mayfield CPF, for his extensive
research efforts.

•

William P. Parker CPF, for his contribution to the section on glazing.

•

Hugh Phibbs for his articles in Picture
Framing Magazine.

•

John Ranes, CPF, GCF for his contribution
to the section on framing stamps.

•

Andrew Nelson Whitehead for the
photographs on papermaking.

•

CREDITS

The following list of products and companies are mentioned in this book. The products are registered to their
respective companies and will carry the ®, ©,or ™, sign
only at the first mention. Thereafter trademarks and brand
names used throughout this book will not carry the trade-
mark or copyright symbol in the text or drawings.

The following companies and products are represented:

3M
    924
    415
Archival Products, L.A.
    Zen Paste
    Insta-Hinge
    Insta-Mend Kit
Art-Sorb
Bookkeeper Preservation Technologies, Inc.
Crescent Cardboard Co.
    Archival Photomount Board
    BriteCores
    Rag Mat 100
    Perfect Mount
Dupont
    Mylar D
Frame Tek, Inc.
    RabbetSpace
    FrameSpace
Fuji Photo Film, USA Inc.
    Fujicolor
Ilford Photo
    Ilfochrome Classic (Cibachrome)
Kodak
    Ektacolor
    Kodacolor
Lineco Inc.
    See-Thru Mounting Strips
    L-Velopes
Neschen
    Filmoplast P90
Nielsen & Bainbridge
    Artcare
Opaline
Puffy
Seal Products Inc.
    ColorMount
Skum-X
Specialty Tapes
    Framer's Tape II
Teledyne
Vicki Schober Co.
    ArtSaver Archival Mounting Strips
Wei T'o Associates Inc.
    Wei T'o
    Good News

CONTENTS

GIVING ADVICE

From the beginning of taking each framing order, be on the lookout for warning signs of potential problems. If dangers are dealt with at this stage, it may save the framer and the customer unnecessary aggravation later. For example:

Will the piece hang in a place that will harm it?

The bathroom; too much humidity

Over the fireplace; soot, heat and cold

Outside walls; colder/damper than interior walls

It is easy to ask the customer while she is choosing mouldings and matboards, "Where will the art hang? In the bathroom? Over the fireplace? At the beach house? In a sunny room?" This can give clues as to what advice should be given the customer and what materials and methods should be used when framing the art.

THE FRAMER'S LIABILITY

How responsible is the framer for conserving the customers' art? Many customers perceive the framer as an expert and rely on the framer's judgement to use the best conservation materials and techniques currently available.

The framer may be legally responsible. Depending on regional, state and federal laws, the framer may be held liable because he/she provides professional services and the assumption could be drawn that the framer "should know better".

To maximize your protection, the work order should state clearly what methods will be employed and the customer should sign in agreement – especially if they reject conservation methods. It is important for the customer to realize that non-conservation methods may cause damage to the art or cause it to depreciate in value.

Whether conservation framing is part of your usual framing practices or not–consider special insurance. Your general business insurance may not cover loss or damage to customer artwork while it is being handled in your workshop. Framers should get advice from an attorney regarding their liability from damage caused by accidents and by deterioration due to methods and materials.

Some framers use only conservation framing materials and techniques in their shops. If a customer insists that she wants her art dry or wet mounted or treated in a non-conservation manner, the customer is asked to sign a release form or disclaimer.

FRAME WORK ORDER

NAME

SP

PHONE

DATE / /

QTY   FRAME   PRICE/FOOT   AMOUNT

CHP   LINER

SIZE

SEE SPECIAL
INSTRUCTIONS ATTACHED

CUSTOMER ELECTED NOT TO
USE CONSERVATION PROCEDURES

DEPOSIT

ITEM   VALUE

ACCEPTED AND AGREED TO

DATE PROMISED
CLAIM CHECK

While disclaimers do not necessarily absolve the framer of liability, they are designed to discourage lawsuits. Ask the customer to sign a brief and simple statement saying that even though the merits of conservation framing were explained, she decided against it. This can be printed onto the bottom of a work order form. The language should be simple and non-threatening, such as, "Even though conservation framing was offered and explained to me, I have decided against it." Next to this statement there should be a line where the customer can sign and date it. This prevents a customer from later claiming that there was a misunderstanding.

The framer should also get a signed release form from the customer when repairing the artwork or doing anything that places the art at risk. It can be used to prove the customer's consent in the event that something does go wrong during the risky procedure and the framer is later sued.

Use release statements judiciously and word them carefully. Too many disclaimers and harsh warnings make customers nervous. A simple "Accepted and agreed to" with a signature and date on the work order can clarify the work and risk.

Carefully analyze the condition of the art when it is received. Make this inspection a part of every order taken into the shop. The framer should not be responsible for damage caused by other framers or handlers of the customer's work, nor for inherent flaws.

Check for acid burns, tears, creases, insects or any other kinds of damage, and show the customer anything discovered. If the artwork is severely damaged or needs treatment by a specialist, let the customer know immediately. If the framer fails to mention these things during the initial framing counter discussion, the customer might assume the damage occurred in the shop. Keep a record of the condition of the artwork and note any apparent damage. Keep forms permanently filed. See the Appendix for the form "Record of Condition Sheet".

THE FRAMER'S CAPABILITIES

Never tackle conservation or restoration techniques beyond individual ability level. Unless the framer happens to be a conservator, restoration is a time-consuming and dangerous craft requiring particular skills and a knowledge of science. If trying a new conservation technique, practice on sample art pieces or papers in the shop. Never attempt a new technique on a customer's artwork. Practice makes perfect, and perfection is essential when working on customer artwork.

Be realistic about your abilities, and seek a professional conservator when necessary. Often a local art museum will have a recommendation or check the list in the Appendix at the back of this book.

VALUE

The long-debated question in framing is which artworks deserve conservation treatment and which do not? Can the framer judiciously determine which artworks should be conserved? Surveys conducted by leading trade magazines show that most framers actually make on-the-spot decisions about each and every order. This one deserves to be conserved ... this one doesn't. Generally, their criteria are: originality; monetary worth or investment value; sentimental value; historical importance; and/or simply importance to the customer.

Considering the overwhelming number of lawsuits today, haphazardly judging the value of artwork places the framer in needless jeopardy. A framer is unable to forecast whether today's trash will become tomorrow's hot new collectible. For instance, maybe a framer thinks that a poster, a child's drawing, or an inexpensive print by a local artist are all valueless. The framer feels it's safe to dry mount them. A few years later the child becomes president, the poster becomes a collector's item and the artist becomes internationally renowned. Now all three "valueless" works are valued – and the decision not to conserve them was made by the framer. The framer could be held responsible for diminishing whatever value these pieces might have.

While preserving artwork in "mint condition" is very important for one-of-a-kind images, it is equally vital for multiple image artwork, like limited-edition prints. In the future resale market, the properly conserved ones will be the most valuable.

WHO DECIDES?

The customer is the owner of the artwork, and the ultimate value of the piece can be determined only by her. Value is personal and has little to do with actual cost. The primary value of any piece of artwork can be put into one of three categories:

    1. Sentimental
    2. Investment
    3. Decorative

The choice of category is up to the customer – not the framer. Sentimental and Investment pieces should be conservation framed, while Decorative pieces can be handled in any fashion.

Discuss conservation options with *every* customer. An educated customer can make informed decisions about her artwork. After explaining the purpose and the cost of conservation framing, the customer chooses which method she prefers.

PAPER. Thin sheets of interwoven cellulose fibers. The cellulose fibers can be obtained from many plants, but wood and cotton are the most common in modern papermaking.

PAPYRUS. Sheets of woven reeds once used as a writing surface, now seen most often by framers as a painting surface for Egyptian art.

PARCHMENT. A writing material made from the skin of sheep. Modern "parchments" are commercially-finished, translucent papers.

pH. The measure of acidity or alkalinity in a substance. The logarithmic scale ranges from 0 acid to 14 alkaline, with the neutral point being 7.

PRESSURE-SENSITIVES. Adhesive tapes or films that attach to a surface when pressure is applied to them. They are not reversible without the use of solvents.

RAG BOARD. A board made of 100% cotton used for matting or mounting or for artwork.

SIZING. A gelatinous mixture used as a sealer or filler in papermaking. It strengthens the paper and reduces water penetration. Some sizings, such as alum-rosin, are no longer in use because they make paper acidic.

SOLANDER BOX. An airtight storage box used by conservators.

STARCH PASTE. An adhesive made from wheat or rice starch mixed with water.

UV-FILTERING. Designed to block the invisible ultraviolet light that is damaging to artwork, usually defined as rays in the 300-400 nanometer range.

VELLUM. A writing material which was originally produced from the skins of calves, goats and lambs. Modern "vellum" is made from treated paper.

WET CUTTING. A technique used in making paper hinges. The paper fibers are torn along a creased, moistened line which produces soft, feathered edges.

WINDOW MAT. A matboard with a window cut out to allow the artwork to be seen. The top mat in a mat package.

ZEOLITES. Synthesized silicates chemically engineered to serve as molecular traps or cages. Added to some matboards and paper products to trap and neutralize pollutants.

CHAPTER 3

PAPER AND BOARDS

ESSENTIAL KNOWLEDGE
PAPER • PAPYRUS • VELLUM • PARCHMENT

Knowledge of how paper and boards are made is required to understand buckles, wrinkles, cockling, and warping, and how paper and boards react during framing procedures and while in a frame over long periods of time, in various environmental conditions.

Art on paper accounts for the majority of work brought into framers. Reproductions, posters, limited edition prints, photographs, original sketches, drawings and prints, watercolors, pastels, collages, letters, documents, postcards, baseball cards – the list is endless. All these are made of either paper (cotton, wood or other pulp), papyrus or animal skins. Once you can identify exactly what you are working with you can better judge the best method of handling it.

The history of paper will not only be helpful and educational, the information can be used to explain conservation techniques and materials to customers.

Mat and mount boards are made of layers of paper, so the story of paper explains both products. Paper and boards are so common in daily existence that there is a tendency to think of it as part of nature, like the air, water, rocks and trees. However, paper is man-made. Few inventions, other than the wheel and the printing press, have had as profound an impact on culture as paper.

PAPER
The word "paper" comes from the Egyptian word Pa-Prro, the Greek word papyros and the Latin word papyrus. Even though paper and papyrus have both been used as writing materials, they are quite different.

To be classified as paper, the raw material must come from fibers that have been beaten until the individual filaments are separated in a pulp. The fibers are suspended in water to release the cellulose that holds the macerated fibers together. Cellulose is a polysaccharide that comes from the wall cells of plants. All plants contain cellulose. The fibers are pulled from the water using a sieve-like screen, leaving a sheet of matted fiber on top of the screen. When it dries, the result is a sheet of paper.

Throughout history, the fibers from which cellulose has been extracted reads like the recipe for a witch's brew: rags, wasps' nests, fish nets, ropes, tree bark, corn husks, pine cones, potatoes, beans, tulips and horse chestnuts; today, wood, cotton and linen are the most common.

PAPYRUS
Papyrus is woven from reeds, not pulped and molded, so it cannot be considered true paper. Papyrus is a tall marsh plant that grows profusely along the Nile river. In approximately 3,000 B.C., at the beginning of the great Egyptian dynasties, it was discovered that the inner bark of this plant could be made into sheets that were ideal to write upon. The thin inner bark strips were peeled off and laminated to one another to form larger sheets or scrolls. The sheets are built up in layers, in much the same way as a carpenter makes laminated wood. The problem with papyrus as a

Profile of a matboard

surface or face paper

core

backing or lining paper

Rag matboard

solid throughout

How Mat & Mount Boards are Made

Mat and mount boards are made from layers of paper – that is why the history of paper is so important to understanding boards. Layers of paper are pasted (called laminated in the paper industry) together and pressed until they form a sheet the desired thickness and strength.

In the paper industry, paper is measured in points or weight but in the framing industry board thickness is often referred to as plies – 1 ply, 2 ply, 14 ply, etc. Unfortunately, ply measurement is not consistent from one manufacturer to another and sometimes even from one board to another, but it does give you a clue about the board.

The plies may refer to the number of layers of paper which have been pasted together. A sheet of regular matboard is a 14 ply board because it consists of 14 layers of paper pasted together.

Most matboards consist of a surface sheet, core layers, and a backing or lining paper. Rag matboards are made by pasting thick sheets of cotton boards together.

How Rag Matboard is Made

The process for making rag board sheets is the same as for making fine papers. Rag board begins before cottonseed is processed, when short fibers left on the seeds are removed during a two-stage process that yields cotton linters. To make cotton linter pulp, bales of cotton linters are opened, pressure cooked, washed, and mildly bleached.

The pulp then goes through a series of centrifugal cleaners to further purify it, removing any fine dirt that may still be present.

Color can be added to rag board pulp during processing. To maintain the highest level of conservation quality, only permanent, lightfast, natural pigments can be used. This results in soft tones such as gray, beige, tan and various creams and whites.

The pulp is transferred to a tile holding chest before being pumped to the headbox of the paper machine. There the pulp is diluted to 5% fiber and 95% water before starting its journey down the rotating wire of the Fourdrinier paper machine.

Water is suctioned through the wire from below as the paper forms, traveling with a gentle side-to-side shaking, toward the dryer section of the machine.

Rag matboards are made by laminating (pasting) thick sheets of cotton boards together to create the 4-ply and 8-ply boards most often used by framers.

CHAPTER 4

HOW PAPER ART IS DAMAGED

Special care should be taken to prevent art on paper from soiling, tearing, creasing, staining and deteriorating. Unfortunately, many paper works do not endure the ravages of time, including atmospheric pollutants, an insufficiency or an overabundance of humidity, inherent or neighboring acids, light, mold, insects and general mistreatment.

Recycling is a natural process. It is a law of nature for once-living materials to eventually return to their natural primary compounds: carbon dioxide, water, oxygen, and other substances. Items made from plants and animals eventually decay. Environmental conditions–light, temperature, humidity and pollutants in the air–accelerate this recycling process. Even high quality papers are vulnerable to deterioration.

To remain as fresh and as beautiful as the day of publication or creation, art must be hermetically-sealed, flat, in a temperature controlled vault. Of course, this is unrealistic for most art lovers and the process would leave picture framers with little to do.

THE NATURE OF PAPER

Anything that was once living, such as paper, contains water. Paper is made from a slurry solution that is 90 percent water and 10 percent fiber. After drying and pressing, paper still has approximately 6 percent of its weight in water.

Paper is hygroscopic, meaning it absorbs moisture like a sponge. As the paper absorbs water, it swells up. Different materials change at different rates and in different ways and to different degrees. So a mixed media collage made from a variety of materials can have a virtual tug-of-war going on.

Paper swells more in the direction of its grain. Moisture is absorbed between the fibers, making them fatter. A machine-made paper will swell in one direction and not the other because of its distinct grain. A handmade paper will enlarge in both directions because the fibers do not have a grain and are intertwined.

To determine which way the grain is running in the paper, flex it gently. It is easier to bend paper in the direction of the grain than going against it or tear it. Paper tears more easily with the grain than against it. Obviously, this is not to be tested on customer art, but do try it with the conservation framing papers that are used in the shop.

ENEMIES OF ART ON PAPER

Cockling
Humidity
Mold & Mildew
Foxing
Insects
Acids
Light
Air Pollution
Heat
Improper Handling
Inherent Flaws
Damage By Prior Framing

Natural Enemies of Art on Paper

Cockling

When art on paper has absorbed moisture from the air, expanding the sheet in one direction more than another, it is said to be "cockled". When cockling occurs, the art appears wavy inside of the frame, instead of laying flat.

The tendency for paper to cockle is natural and should not be considered damage. It should not be stopped by stretching or mounting the art. It is unrealistic and inappropriate to expect paper art to be perfectly flat all of the time. If not severe, cockling should be accepted as is.

The severity of cockling depends on the type of paper and the medium used. For instance, if an artist paints a watercolor on a lightweight paper that is not stretched, the painted area will expand while the unpainted area remains the same. If the painting is centered on the paper the sheet will be bowl shaped. To avoid this problem, watercolorists should pre-stretch their papers to their maximum size before painting. However, many artists do not properly prepare their papers and framers are often presented with badly cockled watercolors.

Severe cockling, going from one extreme to another, can be visually distracting and can break down the paper's fibers. See the chapter on projects for special handling of excessively cockled watercolors.

Humidity

In addition to cockling, high humidity has multiple damaging effects on art. When humidity is high, light damage occurs more rapidly, air pollution is more pronounced and damaging chemical reactions can occur.

When heat or light are present, airborne oxides of sulfur and nitrogen (which come from the combustion of fossil fuels), combine with the water in the paper producing sulfuric and nitric acids that attack the cellulose fibers. These acids gradually break down the paper through a process called acid hydrolysis. The fibers break down into shorter and shorter chains, until the paper loses its strength and becomes brittle. The rate of hydrolysis is faster when there is excessive moisture.

In addition, high humidity creates an environment that is ideally suited for biological attacks from mold, mildew, insects and other environmental pests. It also creates an environment that may promote foxing.

To adequately conserve the art, it is best to keep the relative humidity in the frame below 60 percent. This can be done by controlling the moisture in the surrounding air by using air-conditioning, a dehumidifier or a fan.

Relative humidity is the ratio of the quantity of water present in the air to the greatest amount possible at a given temperature. When water evaporates, water molecules dissolve into air molecules. The amount of water that the air can hold depends on the air temperature. Warm air holds more water than cold air. Air that is holding all of the water that it can is said to be "saturated".

At room temperature (74°F), one pound of air can hold 18/1,000 pound of water. This is absolute humidity. If at the same temperature that one pound of air held 9/1,000 pound of water, half as much as it can hold, the relative humidity of the air would be 50 percent.

To get a general measure of humidity, try using a relative humidity indicator card. This is a flat card impregnated with cobalt salts. The card changes color in relationship to the relative humidity. In some cases, a framer may want to put this card on the back of a frame package. The card is not precise, but it does give an indication of moisture level inside of the frame.

Proper framing helps prevent moisture infiltration. If the art will be in a high-humidity environment, back the frame with polyester and seal it so that it is airtight. This will reduce the chance moisture will seep in.

Silica gel impregnated in paper or in granules can be put inside of an airtight frame. Silica gel is an inert chemical substance that is able to absorb water vapor and serves as a drying agent. If the frame is sealed, the silica gel will work for a long time.

One easy-to-use product that is designed to actually control humidity levels within the frame is called Artsorb®. Sold as beads, or even better for framers, as sheets that can be placed inside frames, Artsorb maintains 50% relative humidity by absorbing and releasing moisture as required by the environment.

Mold and Mildew

Mold is a fungus. It is three-dimensional, hairy and is often green or black. Green is usually penicillium, and aspergillus is usually black or blackish. Mildew is the beginning of mold. It can usually be smelled before it can be seen. Mold grows when the relative humidity exceeds 70 percent. Heat causes it to grow even more rapidly.

The impact of mold is that it digests cellulose. It can cause the leaves of a book to stick together and can eventually destroy paper art. To prevent mold, maintain the relative humidity at 60 percent by using a dehumidifier or air-conditioner.

To treat mold that has developed, take the art out of the high humidity environment and let it dry out. Drying out the art will not kill the mold spores, but will stop their growth. Mold cannot grow unless the relative humidity is higher than 70 percent, so, if it is certain that the art will never again be in a high humidity environment, it doesn't need to be fumigated. Fumigation is required to kill the spores. Since fumigation chemicals are toxic, they are best handled by professional conservators.

Often, mold can be removed after it has been dried. Do not try to brush off the mold before it is dry, as this may grind the wet mold into the paper, permanently staining it.

Foxing

Foxing looks different from mold. It looks like reddish-brown freckle stains and it isn't hairy. While it is disfiguring, it isn't aggressively destructive like mold.

Though conservators debate over what actually causes foxing, most tend to agree that the real problem comes from metal salts, such as copper and iron, that may have been present in the water when the paper was manufactured.

Some conservators believe that foxing is the result of a chemical reaction in the paper between metallic salts and the by-products of fungal growth. Another group believes that the metal salts react with something in the paper itself. The evidence is still inconclusive.

Foxing develops in an environment with high relative humidity. Under low-moisture conditions, it doesn't seem to happen. Treatment for foxing usually involves some type of bleaching, which requires the services of a professional conservator.

Insects

Insects are very sneaky and their attack on a work may not be recognized until there is full-scale damage or infestation. Insects feed on paste, sizing, wood pulp, cellulose fibers, mold and even the artist's medium. They will eat holes in the artwork and their excrement can stain paper. The most common insects affecting artwork are silverfish, book lice, wood worms, termites, and cockroaches.

Silverfish are carrot-shaped wingless insects that have silvery, scaled bodies. They move rapidly and are particularly active at night or in warm, dark areas. They feed on starch, animal sizing, cellulose, and they particularly like bleached wood pulp paper. Silverfish can completely devour artwork.

Book lice are very tiny, mite-like creatures. They have white or brown semi-transparent bodies and live in damp areas. They feed on mold, starch, organic glue, cloth, silk and leather.

Wood worms are wood-boring insects that infest art in highly humid areas. The worms are pale, cream-colored, and will tunnel through wood, board and paper for as long as five years.

Termites are pale, wingless, soft-bodied insects. They eat through paper as well as wood.

Cockroaches are brown, nocturnal insects that like dark, warm, damp areas. They can cause surface damage to parchment, paper, fabric and any adhesives or painting media that contain sugar.

Infestation of any of these insects should be treated by a paper conservator or a certified exterminator.

Be careful when opening an antique frame or customer's framed work that may have been stored in a place which encourages insects such as the basement, garage etc. Open the piece outside your workshop. Should these insects get into your stock of matboards or mouldings you will need an exterminator to be rid of them.

ACIDS

Acid is what eats away at the cellulose in paper, turning it yellow and causing it to embrittle. The term "acid-free" can be confusing. It may mean the item is without acid or the acid level has been neutralized. The term is used to mean both things in various conservation framing products. The term acid-free did not originate in the framing industry. It refers to a chemical change when a buffering agent is used, which attacks the "free acids" -- those beyond the limit of neutral, thereby creating a neutral condition. It does not mean that there are no acids present.

There are few things in this world that are truly "acid-free". The *only* true naturally acid-free matboard is pure 100% cotton rag board. Even then, the board is acid-free only when it is first manufactured. During its lifetime, it can absorb airborne acids. This is why it is important to control the environment around the art.

Acidity and alkalinity is measured on a pH scale which ranges from 1 to 14. The neutral point is 7.0. At this point,

There are a variety of products on the market that can be used to test the pH of art or matboard. One such product is a pH pen. Because it has a permanent dye, it should not be used on customer artwork; but it can be a useful exercise for framers to try with various papers in the shop. To use the pen, simply moisten a spot on the paper. Then rub the pen on that spot. The color of the mark will match a color on the pH chart that comes with the pen, indicating whether the paper is acidic, neutral or alkaline.

Paper can be naturally neutral or chemically neutralized. Although a paper may be acid-free or have a pH of between six and eight, it may become increasingly acidic over time.

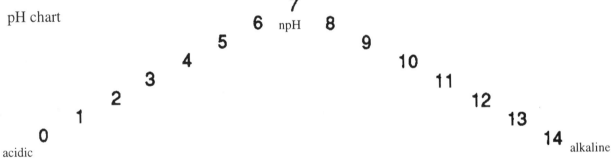

pH chart

0 1 2 3 4 5 6 7 npH 8 9 10 11 12 13 14

acidic   alkaline

the material is neither acidic nor alkaline. The lower the number, the higher the acidity. The higher the number, the higher the alkalinity. The difference between numerals is significant because the scale is logarithmic which means each pH change of one indicates a change of 10 times in the acidity or alkalinity measurement. As a frame of reference, at pH 10 is soap. At pH 3 is vinegar. Conservation materials should be at pH 6.5 - 8.5.

Buffering compounds such as calcium carbonate are added to rag board and high-quality conservation papers, enabling them to neutralize acids they come in contact with. To make calcium carbonate, limestone is chemically converted into microcrystals. Small amounts (two to three percent) are added to the paper pulp.

Generally, conservation framers use papers that have a pH between 6.5 and 8.5 with 1 to 3 percent alkaline reserve.

LIGHT

Most of the other damage to art is relatively insignificant in comparison to the damage caused by light. It is the most pervasive and most difficult damage to avoid.

Light will cause the paper and the artist's medium to change by fading, changing color, altering chemicals in paper and paint, and degrading cellulose. The extent of the damage depends on the intensity of the light and the length of exposure.

Light is measured in wavelengths. The most harmful type of light is the shorter wavelengths (higher frequencies) in the light spectrum: invisible ultraviolet light. This type of light is found in fluorescent light, sunlight and black lights. These lights cause the greatest damage because they contain the highest energy levels.

Longer wavelengths (shorter frequencies) of light, such as incandescent light produced by household light bulbs, cause less damage, but can still be a problem. While they cast

very little ultraviolet light, their heat can be damaging, especially if they are too close to the art.

No matter what the source, light is energy and when combined with water or certain chemicals, it can produce a photosensitized reaction. Light promotes the breakdown of lignin in paper causing the breakdown of the long cellulose chains into shorter and shorter fibers until the paper is brittle and tan colored.

Strong light also reacts severely with some dyes, inks and paints, causing them to bleach-out, fade away, darken or discolor. Some light-sensitive media include: paints used in hand-colored prints, thin watery inks used in Japanese prints, watercolors, pastels, some photographs, felt-tip and ballpoint pen inks, as well as modern inks made with aniline dyes. Great care should be taken with several types of color copies and line printer inks and thermograph copies.

Paper should be displayed under the lowest practical light levels. Direct morning or afternoon sunlight must be avoided. Spotlights and picture lights should not be aimed directly at artwork. Ultraviolet-filtering glazing can provide some protection from light damage. Attaching filters to flu-

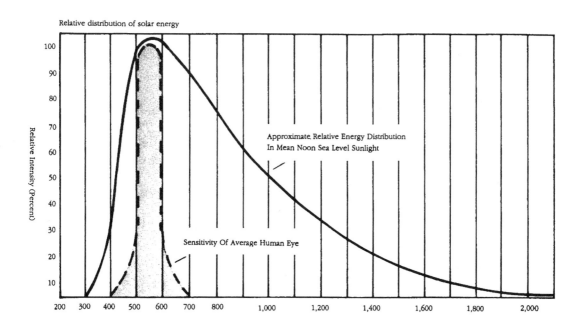

orescent and halogen lights will help reduce damage to artwork on display.

AIR POLLUTION

Another environmental problem is air pollution. The more polluted a city is, the greater the problems. Sulfur dioxide, nitrogen dioxide and hydrogen sulfide are by-products of smoke and burning fossil fuels, such as coal, furnace oil and gasoline. When combined with the moisture and oxygen in the air, they produce acids that attack and destroy paper. Airborne dirt is also harmful to paper because it carries absorbed pollutants. In addition to disfiguring the art, dust particles can be abrasive to the art's surface.

Airborne gases and dirt seep into inadequately sealed frames, coming in through cracks and seams. These acids can destroy artists' pigments, as well as embrittle, discolor and break down the paper's fibers.

It's difficult to escape air pollution. Air-conditioning can help regulate the humidity and deter further damage. Deacidification (Chapter 7) may also help. Probably the best defense against air pollution is to use framing materials that contain buffering agents like calcium carbonate and to adequately seal the backs of the frames.

Papers, boards and backings have been developed containing "zeolites" which are molecular traps that absorb pollutants. Although these may prove to be very useful in the battle against air pollution, their use in framing is new and several concerns remain. If the molecular traps attract and hold the pollution, will they get full? Will the traps hold the pollution forever? Will the active chemical react with other chemicals in artists' paint or photographic chemicals? Some conservators refer to this type of product as an aggressive method. These boards, backing papers and related products may eventually prove to be very helpful in highly polluted areas.

HEAT

Paper produced from wood pulp deteriorates much more rapidly when exposed to heat. It accelerates the conversion of lignin into sulfuric acid causing yellowing, embrittlement and general deterioration.

Research shows that the lower the temperature in which the art is displayed, the longer it will last. For example, if paper is kept at 40°F, it will survive twice as long as paper that is kept at 50°F. Paper that is kept at 50°F will have a life twice as long as paper kept at 60°F and so on.

The best practical temperature for artwork is 70 F. Art should not hang on walls that radiate heat, such as above fireplaces or radiators. High temperatures combined with high relative humidity inside of a frame may result in mold growth. Abrupt changes in temperatures may result in condensation inside the frame which will also cause mold growth and induce foxing.

IMPROPER HANDLING

Of all the dangers facing artwork, handling and storage are among the greatest threats. Improper handling causes tears, nicks, creases, and folds. Poor judgement may result in trimming of margins and fingerprints.

Handling of artwork should be minimized. When artwork must be handled, first wash hands with non-scented soap and water; dry thoroughly. No hand creams or lotions. Although hands may look clean, they are naturally oily and contain perspiration salts. While working with the art, avoid touching your face.

Protect the surface of the art. Do not run the fingers or slide sheets of paper across the media. Mezzotints, pastel drawings and silk screens can easily chip or scratch. Never lay these works face down on the work surface.

Do not pick up paper art between three fingers – this will leave a "v"-shaped dent that may not flatten. Lift artwork with two hands. Avoid rolling it. Rolling not only breaks down the fibers in the paper, but may dent, tear or crease the paper and bend the media into a cupped shape which may later chip off.

INHERENT FLAWS

Discolored and brittle newsprint, faded photographs, watercolors and color copies, art done on construction paper, collages done with poor adhesives–many pieces cannot be saved, although some can be controlled.

In addition to destructive elements that may exist within the paper, artists may use media or mixtures of media that cause damage by bleeding into or eating through the paper. There is little, if anything, one can do about the quality of the artwork that is presented to the framer. In severe cases, refer the customers to a paper conservator.

DAMAGE CAUSED BY PRIOR FRAMING

Often there is damage caused by improper handling, especially in pieces framed many years ago, before conservation materials were widely available and commonly used by picture framers. Mats were introduced in the 1920s so many earlier pieces were not distanced from the glass resulting in extensive damage: folds, ripples, and adhesion to the glass.

MATTING

Old wood pulp matboards are acidic. If this type of board was used, eventually the art absorbed some of the acid in the mat surrounding it, resulting in a yellowish-brown burn line along the edges of the bevel or at any point where the mat has touched the art.

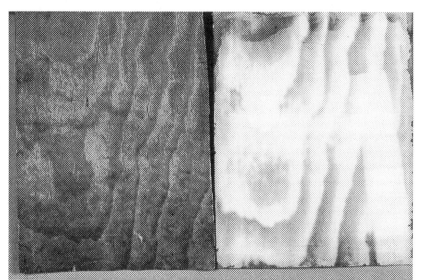

Plywood filler board.   *Back side of a photograph*
The plywood at the left has caused an acid burn on the back of a photograph. The outline of the work order can be seen on the far right.

At one time is was acceptable to use a standard matboard in conjunction with rag boards; this is no longer true. It is now known that even though the acidic boards may not touch the art, the acids in the wood pulp can migrate within the frame causing deterioration of the artwork.

Artwork should be kept at least 1/2" from the edge of its mat. If it touches the edge of the frame it will buckle.

HINGING

DO NOT USE masking tape, brown wrapping tape, pressure-sensitive tapes, cellophane tapes, rubber cement and synthetic and animal-based glues – they stain artwork and are not reversible. Attempts at removing old adhesive require extreme caution and best left to a paper conservator. Unless the old adhesives affect enjoyment of the design area fo the artwork, leave them alone and hide them with matting.

BACKING BOARD

Often, artwork is stained because it was backed with wood, regular corrugated cardboard or regular matboard. Regular corrugated cardboard will produce striped acid burns on artwork. Sheets of thin plywood were used during the late 1800s. The wood degrades, imparting acids and staining anything it contacts. Often a complete image of the backing board, complete with woodgrain and knotholes, is burned onto the back of artwork that has been pressed against it.

MOULDING

Acids in wood moulding can migrate onto the paper, causing yellowing and brittle edges in the art. Artwork should be kept at least 1/2" away from the rabbet of the moulding. In addition, wood mouldings should be lined with polyvinyl tape, rag paper, or frame sealing tape.

Use Frame Sealing Tape by Lineco®

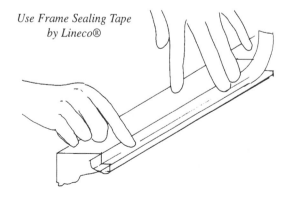

GLAZING

Artwork should never be placed in direct contact with glass. Glass is a poor conductor of energy, which means that it changes temperature more slowly than the surrounding atmosphere.

In cool rooms which are warming (the period before and after sunrise) glass will remain cool while the temperature of the air in the room rises. The cooler surface of the glass will cause the moisture in the air to condense on both surfaces of the glass. This condensation moisture can damage artwork if it is touching the glass. In the short run, absorbed moisture can create or increase cockling in artwork. In the long run, it can significantly increase the chance of the development of foxing and mold. If airspace is provided, with matting or spacers, the condensation can harmlessly evaporate as the glass temperature reaches air temperature.

A strange phenomenon, called photo-transference, occurs on some framed pieces that are directly against glass, or sometimes even on pieces that have a mat. An image of the art is transferred to the inside of the glass. The image seems to disappear when the glazing is washed only to reappear after it dries. The image is actually permanently "baked" on the glazing. Photo-transference is caused by gases inside the frame, often from inks, paints, and other chemicals in the art. While this is not initially damaging to the art, pieces that show these tendencies should be aired out and spaced away from the glass in future framing.

Drawings done with powdery mediums, such as pastels, charcoals, chalks and heavy graphites, are susceptible to flaking and can be severely damaged if placed in direct contact with glazing. In addition, static from acrylic glazing tends to lift soft media from the paper. Use a double mat or spacer mats with loose media to prevent any contact with the glazing.

While the framer cannot control the material that the art is made of or the external environment it will be subjected to, framers can control the art's immediate, physical environment – that is, the materials inside of the frame package. These materials have a lot to do with the how long the art will last and in what condition.

If airspace is provided, with matting or spacers, the condensation can harmlessly evaporate as the glass temperature reaches air temperature.

Drawings done with powdery mediums, such as pastels, charcoals, chalks and heavy graphites, are susceptible to flaking and can be severely damaged if placed in direct contact with glazing.

CHAPTER 5

SELECTING MATERIALS

BOARDS • ADHESIVES • GLAZING • SOLVENTS • ETC.

HOW TO CHOOSE MATERIALS

Conservation materials are those products that do their job without harming the art in any way. They should remain stable for many years, and not develop harmful properties over time. Unfortunately, some products eventually lose whatever conservation properties made them initially desirable, and are not suitable for conservation framing.

Numerous fine-quality conservation products are currently on the market and new ones appear frequently. Become familiar with a wide variety of conservation materials and stock a selection of them in the framing shop. Framing projects are often complicated and may require several methods or techniques.

Always purchase conservation materials from reliable framing suppliers. Do not substitute seemingly like or better products from other markets–surgical tape belongs in the doctors office, not the frame shop. Read the description in distributors' catalogs and on the product labels. The product should be described as intended for use in conservation framing.

Do not be fooled by marketing words that sound good, such as "acid-free" or "archival". Although these are fine qualifiers, there may be more to it than that: Is it totally reversible? Is a solvent required? While words may imply that the product is non-damaging, acid-free and reversible, do not assume that just from the use of the words. Before buying such a product, ask three important questions:
1. What is the intended use of this product? Be sure that it is designed to meet individual needs.
2. What is the product made of? The manufacturer can give a list of the basic ingredients in the product.
3. What is the supporting data? The manufacturer should be able to show scientific tests done on the product that substantiate conservation claims being made about it.

Information can be obtained from distributors, ads in trade magazines and directly from the manufacturers. Trade shows are a great place to talk directly with manufacturers.

All methods and procedures must be totally reversible, leaving no residue or impressions.

To be properly conservation framed, all materials inside the frame package must either be naturally acid-free or treated to be acid-free.

MAT AND MOUNT BOARDS

Boards used in conservation framing must be made from either cotton or chemically processed wood pulp. In ads and promotional brochures, rag or alpha cellulose is used to describe conservation boards

The term 100 percent rag means that the paper is made of 100 percent cotton or cotton linters—not rags. Some hand-made papers may be made from cotton threads or scraps of cotton, but matboards are made from the lint removed from the cottonseed.

Matboards made from cotton are naturally acid-free; buffering is added to protect the board from acid or pollution it may come in contact with over time. No lignins are present in cotton.

Matboard called alpha cellulose board is made from wood pulp that has been cooked and digested, a process which frees the pulp of the lignins that made it acidic. After the pulp has been processed, it is basically the same as rag board. Though the fibers in the two boards are different, they are both equally stable and equally suitable for use in conservation framing. The difference is in the chemicals used to process the boards and the level of buffering required. Alpha cellulose boards are always buffered, which may not be suitable when framing alkaline-sensitive artwork such as animal-based items and some photographs.

The acidity or alkalinity of a paper is measured on a pH logarithmical scale that goes from 0 to 14. The neutral point is 7.0. At this point, the material is neither acidic nor alkaline. The lower the number, the higher the acidity. The higher the number the higher the alkalinity. A pH between 6.5 and 8.5 is desirable for papers that are plant based; this is the pH range that buffered boards are designed to maintain. However, some studies have shown that some animal-based items such as silk, wool, leather, skins and some photography processed with animal-based products prefer a slightly acidic environment. They do not fare well in high alkaline mats or boards with alkaline reserves. Non-buffered boards are best for these items.

Sizing fills in the pores of the paper's fibers so that the paper is easier to write and print on. Some sizings make paper acidic. Today, board and papermakers, especially those making conservation matboards and papers, are using a synthetic, alkaline sizing.

Profile of a matboard

surface or face paper

core

backing or lining paper

Mat & Mount Boards
used for
Conservation Framing

Museum Grade boards
are those with:
- 100% Cotton rag
  solid cotton throughout
  buffered or non-buffered

Conservation Grade
boards are those with:
- Cotton rag core and lining
  paper with alpha cellulose
  surface papers
- Alpha cellulose surface
  paper, core & lining paper

BUFFERING

A buffering compound may be added to the pulp. Buffers cannot be added to papers that have been sized with alum-rosin. Buffering raises the alkaline level of the paper, enabling it to ward-off airborne acids. Calcium carbonate, which is derived from limestone or chalk, is frequently used as a buffer. Small amounts (two to three percent) of these buffering compounds are added to the pulp. The buffers combine chemically with the acids they encounter and neutralize them, making the pulp acid-free. The excess buffering remains in the board creating an "alkaline reserve".

BOARDS FOR WINDOW MATS

The window mat serves two important functions: It is the presentation border for the artwork and it prevents the art from touching the glazing. Since paper artwork expands and contracts with changes in the environment, matting gives the artwork breathing space.

Conservation boards come in various thicknesses, layers or "plies". Four-ply rag board works well for most medium- and small-sized works. However, it may be necessary to use 8-ply for larger works because they are stronger and have more body than 4-ply. Two-ply is too thin for a window mat because it does not provide enough space between the glazing and the art, and it is too weak to use as a backing board.

Definitions of boards can be confusing ...acid-free, museum quality, museum grade, conservation quality, museum conservation quality. Here are the designations selected by the Fine Art Trade Guild (UK), the Institute for Paper conservation (UK), and the American Institute of Conservation for Historic & Artistic Works (US).

MUSEUM BOARDS

Museum board is made of 100 percent cotton. It may be buffered or non-buffered. Boards prior to the late 70s did not have buffering, and many museums still use non-buffered cotton boards. The color range available in museum board is limited because the pigments used must be naturally neutral, fade resistant and able to color cotton evenly. Hydrogen peroxide is used as a bleach. It is harmless and does not pollute the waters or cause health problems in workers.

Cotton rag boards are the matboards virtually all museums world-wide *really* use. They may recommend other boards for storage and fillers but they absolutely use cotton rag for

matting. Cotton rag is a passive product. It has little or no effect on whatever it frames. It contains no active chemicals. It is available buffered, which is best for most kinds of paper art, and also non-buffered, for artwork with special pH needs.

CONSERVATION BOARDS

These boards are made with a rag or purified woodpulp core and have paper surfaces adhered to the core. These surface papers are acid-free and highly fade and bleed resistant. Lining papers on the back are also acid-free. These boards are buffered, providing a pH of about 8.5 and an alkaline reserve of approximately 1 to 3 percent. For conservation framing, this board is nearly as good as 100% rag board.

The boards made from purified woodpulp are sometimes called alpha cellulose boards. Some manufacturers call the boards made from this pulp museum-quality or conservation-quality but they don't call them museum boards (because only rag fits that definition).

CONSERVATION BOARDS WITH MOLECULAR TRAPS

One new type of matboard contains additives called "zeolites", which are "cage molecules" designed to attract, trap, and neutralize a range of pollutants beyond those dealt with by calcium and magnesium carbonate buffers. This product may well be a valuable tool for conservation framing; lab tests have shown promising results. However, there is not yet sufficient real-experience proof of their safety and effectiveness. Some conservators are concerned about the long-term effects of active ingredients like zeolites within the frame package.

FABRIC-COVERED MATS

If a fabric-covered mat is desired, there are many conservation boards that are available already covered with acid-free fabric. If the framer makes a fabric-covered mat, make sure the adhesive used for mounting the fabric, and the fabric itself, meet conservation criteria. If acidity of the fabric is high or unknown, it should be deacidified, if possible (see Chapter 7, Deacidification).

BRITECORES®, BLACK CORES, AND COLOR CORES.

These boards must be qualified by the manufacturer. They are made from chemically processed wood pulp and are saturated with pigment. Check for npH, buffering, and lignin.

Regular or Standard Matboard

This is a wood pulp board manufactured from virgin pulp or recycled pulp. The core may be off-white or white. This board contains lignin, although it is buffered and will remain pH neutral for a period of time. How long the buffering will keep the board neutral is not known. Since the ground wood pulp contains lignins, it will eventually become acidic again as the alkaline reserve is used up. This board is not appropriate for conservation framing.

At one time it was thought that regular matboards could be used in conservation framing, if rag mats or barrier paper separated them from the artwork. Now it is known that acids in the standard matboard can migrate from the board and damage the artwork. Buffering in the standard boards may delay, but cannot prevent this.

Several companies have introduced a non-conservation white core board. Despite its attractive appearance, this is not a conservation board and cannot be used in conservation framing.

Backing Boards

The backing board is the board to which the art is attached. It is also called the support board, substrate or mounting board.

Use the same type of board that was used for the window mat to create the backing board. If the window mat is made from 4-ply rag board, then the backing board must be made from 4-ply rag board. If the art is particularly heavy use an 8-ply for more support.

Do not use filler board materials as backing boards. Always use the same quality board immediately behind the artwork as was used for the window mat.

Filler Boards

The filler board completes the inside of the frame package. It goes behind the backing board and takes up the remaining room in the moulding rabbet providing stability and a barrier from the elements.

Acceptable conservation filler boards are:
- 4ply rag board
- Rag foam center board
- Acid-free foam center board
- Acid-free corrugated board.

Foam Center Board

This board consists of a polystyrene core with paper laminated to both front and back surfaces. It is lightweight, rigid, and resists moisture. The surface papers may be buffered rag, buffered acid-free, or wood pulp. Use the rag or acid-free surfaces in conservation framing. Although the polystyrene center deteriorates if exposed to light, it is considered inert when completely sealed inside of a frame.

Acid-Free Corrugated Board

This board is made of acid-free paper that has been laminated onto a fluted core. As with matboards, there are two kinds made for conservation framing -- one made from cotton, the other from acid-neutralized wood pulp. The acids in these boards have been neutralized so the board has a pH value of 7.5 to 8.0. This board is available in two thicknesses. These boards are usually white or bluish-gray.

While it is a good filler board, it should never be used next to the artwork. The pressure inside the frame could press fluted marks onto the art. Also, do not confuse this board with regular corrugated cardboard, which is lethal for art because it is highly acidic.

Acid-Free Mounting Boards

These boards are double-sided, white acid-free mounting boards. All components are treated with calcium carbonate to be pH neutral. Available in two thicknesses. While not strictly a conservation board, it can be used as a filler board. Some photographers insist on mounting photos on this board because of its smooth, hard surface.

Newsboard, Chipboard and Upson Board

All three are thick, dense boards made of recycled materials and are highly acidic. They should not be used in any way in conservation framing.

CONSERVATION ADHESIVES AND PASTES

Adhesion is what causes two substances to stick together. In conservation framing, adhesives and pastes are used to attach paper hinges to art and backing boards. The various types of hinges serve as bridges between the art and backing board. In conservation framing, use a water based adhesive on anything that touches the art, so that it will be water-reversible. If removal becomes necessary in the future, the paper's sizing helps keep moisture out of the art during rewetting, preventing the paper from staining. Sizing is not designed to resist solvents. If solvents are needed to remove adhesive they tend to spread into the paper, possibly loosening dyes or pigments, or staining the paper.

Look for the following qualities when choosing a conservation adhesive:
- Acid-free
- Strong enough to hold the artwork
- No discoloration
- Water soluble
- Easy to prepare
- Does not attract insects or mold

WHEAT OR RICE STARCH PASTE
Most conservators prefer one of these adhesives. Though there are a variety of "vegetable adhesives" available, wheat and rice starch are the most common. Wheat starch is a little stronger and is more commonly used than rice starch. Wheat starch is used to attach Japanese paper hinges onto the artwork and onto the backing board. The only negative in using wheat or rice paste is that it takes time to make and the paste lasts only three or four days before it begins to spoil.

METHYL CELLULOSE PASTE
This is an organic powder, made from cotton or wood cellulose. It can be purchased from most framing suppliers. Mix it with cold water, following the manufacturer's directions. It can be stored in a jar and does not need to be refrigerated.

Methyl cellulose will not stain and resists mold. It is reversible by moistening with water. As an adhesive for Japanese hinges, methyl cellulose is readily accepted and used in conservation framing. Methyl cellulose paste is not as strong as wheat or rice starch paste.

ZEN PASTE®

This pre-cooked wheat paste comes in a moist ready-to-use form or as freeze dried crystals to mix with water. It is pH neutral, contains fungicide, has a long shelf-life and is water reversible. It is strong enough to hold heavy prints.

HINGES, TAPES AND SUPPORT DEVICES
Some hinges, tapes and mounting devices not only damage the art while they are attached to it but they can ruin the art when attempting to remove them.

It is important to know what potential harm the hinge, tape or mounting device can cause the art either now or in years to come. Anything used to support the art in conservation framing should be reversible, stable and non-damaging. Adhesives are grouped into sections: A, B, & C. Each group is described on the following pages.

Group A: Non-Staining, Acid-Free, Water-Reversible

These adhesive mounting devices can be used in contact with the art. They are reversible with nothing more than water and non-staining. This group also includes independent supports, which hold artwork with no adhesive contact.

JAPANESE PAPERS
These papers, typically made from the white inner bark of young kozo, gampi or mitsumata plants, are the basic material for making all handmade conservation hinges and repair patches. Made in Japan and Korea, these papers are sold in sheets in a variety of weights and finishes. The fibers are interwoven in the paper-making process, making the paper very strong.

Hand torn Japanese paper hinges, with cooked wheat or rice starch paste, is the preferred method of virtually all museum conservators.

Since there are so many weights to choose from, it's best to have several on hand. Buy only high-quality papers. When selecting a Japanese paper for a particular hinge, choose one that is strong, yet thinner than the artwork.

INSTA-HINGE®
Japanese paper impregnated with re-wettable wheat starch paste. Strips 1-1/2 x 24", can be cut or torn into the size needed. Moisten one side of the strip with water and use in the same manner as regular Japanese hinges. These are very easy to use and good for a shop that wants to eliminate time required to cook starch paste.

ArtSaver® MOUNTING STRIPS
This mounting trough is similar to the Mylar mounting strip. The trough is made from 1ply rag board, which is folded along a score line and mounted to the backboard.

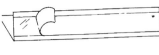

SEE-THRU MOUNTING STRIPS®
Made by Lineco, the strips are made out of Mylar®, 1ply rag board and a neutral pH polyvinyl self-adhesive. Essentially, the art is held in place on a rag board ledge with Mylar, supporting the art onto the backing board without adhesive contact.

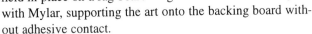

MOUNTING CORNERS
Made from rag paper or Mylar. Available in several sizes. Backed with pressure-sensitive adhesive, they adhere to the backing board easily. Corners are approved by the Library of Congress and are safe for mounting photographs, postcards, memorabilia, clippings, letters, prints and paper items. Most libraries and archives use these corners to mount prints into portfolios or on mounting boards that are in storage.

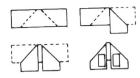

Though archivally-safe, corners may not be able to support the weight of artwork for a long period of time. Gravity causes the art to settle and eventually it may buckle. When using these corners, be careful that the print is not mounted too tightly between the corners and that it has adequate space to expand and contract. If the mat covers a considerable part of the carrier sheet of the artwork the corners will function very well.

GUMMED LINEN OR COTTON TAPE
Although the box may state linen, the tape is more frequently made from a very fine cotton fabric. The tape is coated with a wettable dextrin adhesive similar to that of postage stamps. Because of its thickness, restrict use to art that is thicker than the tape. The cloth on this is very strong, making it useful for heavier artwork.
Author's note: I have used Lineco® Gummed linen tape to float huge paper sculptures.

GUMMED PAPER TAPE
Similar to gummed linen/cotton tape, except it is backed with paper rather than cloth. The paper is coated with a dextrin-based adhesive that can be moistened with water. If used as a hinge to support art, the art must be heavier than the hinge.
This tape is effective for hinging skin documents, bark paintings and resin coated photographs.

Group B: Acid-Free, Clear, Stable, Non-Staining Materials, Not Water Reversible

These tapes may be used in the conservation framing package but should not be used in direct contact with the art because they are permanent.

Although many of these tapes carry an inert, acid-free adhesive, they are not water-reversible. All pressure-sensitive tapes must be removed with solvents. Over time, the adhesives can deteriorate and soak into the paper, causing stains that may be impossible to remove.

Pressure-sensitive tapes are self-adhesive–they are simply placed in position and pressed.

The carrier may be removed with water or with heat, using a tacking iron, but ALL pressure-sensitive tapes require solvents or extreme conservator techniques to remove the adhesive. Often the adhesive is not actually removed, only softened. Residue from the solvent may remain in the paper, which may react with the paper over time. For these reasons, pressure-sensitive tapes should only be used in contact with artwork under very specific, unusual circumstances when other methods have been exhausted.

FILMOPLAST P-90® AND P-91® TAPE
These are neutral pH, pressure-sensitive tapes. Both are buffered with calcium carbonate and are 3/4" wide. The tapes are made so that the adhesive is attached to the carrier sheet by a water infusion process. The carrier sheet can be removed with water, but the adhesive will remain in place, making this tape unsuitable for true conservation hinges because adhesive remains on the artwork.

PRESSURE-SENSITIVE LINEN/COTTON TAPE
Pressure-sensitive linen/cotton tape is strong, acid-free and is easy to apply. This pressure-sensitive tape should not be used in direct contact with art. It is too thick and strong for most artworks and it shrinks when it dries, possibly causing the art to buckle. It can be used to attach window mats to their backing boards.

DOCUMENT REPAIR TAPE
Made be Lineco, this 1" wide tape is designed especially for torn documents. It is pH neutral and non-yellowing. It is permanent and requires a solvent for removal.

HEAT-SET HINGING TAPE
Like pressure-sensitive tapes, this hinging tape and repair tissue is clear, acid-free and non-yellowing, but is not water-reversible. Some are heat-reversible, but will require solvents if heat does not work. When heat or solvents are used the carrier will lift off leaving the adhesive.

Pressure-sensitive tapes and adhesives may state they are archival, stable, non-yellowing, inert, and npH; however, they are not water reversible and in some cases they are not even solvent removable.

Using pressure-sensitive tapes and films in contact with art must be considered a method of last resort, because they are not water-reversible.

FRAMERS TAPE II
This tape is very strong and stable and the carrier sheet is heat removable; however, when heat is applied to remove the carrier sheet, residue of adhesive will be left behind in the paper of the artwork.

ATG #924 and #415
These are double-sided pressure-sensitive tapes that are most often used to attach the dust cover to the back of the frame or attach double mats together. The adhesive is polyvinyl acrylic. It is permanent and it gets stronger as it ages. It may be used in the framing package but not attached to the artwork.

POLYVINYL TAPES
Some examples of these types of tapes are 3M's #810 and #811 tapes. These tapes are strong, stable and clean, but not reversible. The adhesive becomes stronger over time, making it more difficult to remove. Heat and pressure speed up settling. They may be used in the framing package but not attached to the art.

GROUP C   Do NOT Use

DO NOT USE the Following in Conservation Framing

CELLOPHANE TAPE   This tape has a rubber-based adhesive. When exposed to air, the adhesive becomes sticky, oily and yellow.

MASKING TAPE   Highly acidic, rubber-based adhesive, carrier turns brittle, the adhesive becomes gooey and stains.

RUBBER CEMENT   This adhesive is acidic and temporary. It will soak into the paper and stain it.

FILAMENT TAPE   Very acidic, temporary and staining.

BROWN PAPER SEALING TAPE.   It is very acidic.

SURGICAL   Although this is an acrylic adhesive it becomes very soft and melds into the paper.

DUCT TAPE   Don't even think about it.

SOLVENTS

It is best to avoid solvents altogether in conservation framing. A variety of solvents will remove or dissolve newly-applied or old adhesives; they may also dissolve ink and dyes. TEST the artwork in an obscure spot before using.

Any solvent strong enough to dissolve adhesive is potentially dangerous to humans and artwork and should be used according to the manufacturer's directions. Be aware of the solvent's flash points. The flash point is the lowest temperature at which the vapors can ignite if they come in contact with a heat source.

Use solvents in a well-ventilated area, preferably in a spray booth. Avoid breathing vapors and wear rubber gloves to avoid skin contact. Store all solvents in a metal cabinet, away from heat.

ADHESIVE RELEASE.   This solvent contains naphtha, which is a by-product of coal tar distillation. It belongs to the benzol group of solvents. It is highly toxic and should be used only in well-ventilated areas. Adhesive release has a strong odor. Its flash point is below 73°F.

MINERAL SPIRITS.   This is a colorless, volatile solvent, distilled from crude petroleum oils. It is very similar to turpentine. In fact, most paint stores refer to it as "turpentine substitute". It has a mild odor. Its flash point is between 100° to 140°F.

ACETONE.   A lacquer solvent, the principle ingredient in many paint removers. A powerful, volatile chemical which is relatively low in toxicity, but safety precautions should be taken. Flash point is 73°F.

TOLUENE.   Colorless solvent with a characteristic odor. Toluene can be absorbed through the skin. Flash point is 100°F.

GLAZING

Glazing is a term that is used both for glass and acrylic that covers the window mat, protecting the front of the frame package from airborne pollutants. It also provides a window for viewing. The type of glazing chosen significantly affects the appearance of the art, now and in the future. *Please reference the light chart on page 25.*

Radiant energy from the sun is divided into bands (light spectrum) which are defined by their unique wavelength of energy. Part of the band is visible to the human eye, and part is invisible. Except for some inks used in some giclée prints, the visible portion of the light spectrum does not tend to damage artwork, unless exposure is intense and prolonged. The invisible ultraviolet portion of the light spectrum does have an adverse affect on artwork. Ultraviolet light transmits energy into the atoms of the objects it strikes. This energy excites the atoms and transforms them into new substances. In artwork, ultraviolet radiation causes fading and deterioration.

Because light is so damaging to art, manufacturers are now making products that will shield artwork from most of the ultraviolet rays in the 300-400 nanometer range. Until 1997, filtration was limited to 97% of UV rays. Filtration beyond 380 nanometers was thought to result in changes in the perception of the color blue. However, one manufacturer is offering a new product that claims to filter 99% of the UV radiation up to 400 nanometers, with no apparent change in the colors of the artwork.

Glazing with UV-filtering properties is the best for conservation framing. However, it is important to advise customers that UV-filtering does not mean the artwork is completely protected from light damage. Artwork should still be shielded from direct and excessive sunlight. The mere presence of a lite of even regular glass will provide minimal protection against some UV rays.

REGULAR GLASS

This glass is often called Float glass or SSB, single-strength B-grade glass. This is ordinary picture framing glass. Iron content in the product gives it a greenish tone.

PREMIUM GLASS

This is the same as regular glass, except the quality is a little higher. There are no flaws in this glass, and it is very clear. A 2 mil. thickness is available, which is very thin glass that can be used on small- to medium-sized works. 2-mil. is too thin for very large works.

NON-GLARE GLASS

This is regular glass that has had an acid bath. The acid etches the surface so that it breaks up reflected light. All acid is washed from the glass, so it is completely non-acidic and safe for conservation use. Purists may state that scattering the entering light means less light is transmitted to the artwork--hence a distorted view at some angles, especially when the glazing is separated from the artwork. More recently, a higher quality of glass has been manufactured, which has a single-sided acid-etched surface. For conservation purposes it is the same as regular glass.

UV FILTERING CLEAR OR NON-GLARE

These have all of the qualities of the non-filtering varieties, plus a UV-filtering coating. One type of glass has a thin UV-filtering sheet sandwiched inside of the glass. This type can be very difficult to cut.

OPTICALLY-COATED GLASS

This is also called invisible glass. It has an anti-reflective coating that increases transmission of visible light, while minimizing glare. It provides reflection control, even at shadowbox depth. The coating is similar to that used on camera lenses and has the same slightly purple cast.

UV-FILTERING OPTICALLY-COATED GLASS

The same as above, plus a coating or lamination that absorbs ultraviolet rays.

ANTI-REFLECTIVE GLASS

This type of glass provides non-reflective clarity to approximately 1/4" depth through a special process called micro-etching, which is a different process than acid-etching. The micro-etching has the effect of neutralizing reflections. Like the other glass types, it is available with or without UV-filtering. The filtering type is ideal for conservation framing.

"WHITE" GLASS, OR WATER WHITE GLASS

Like anti-reflective glass, this product provides increased light transmission, providing great clarity. It is a low-iron glass, which minimizes the green hue common in picture framing glass. It is available with and without UV-filtering.

ACRYLIC SHEETING

Like regular glass, this material does not filter significant amounts of ultraviolet rays. Some brands make a scratch resistant type. Some plastics may eventually discolor. Approximately half the weight of glass, acrylic is useful when weight is a consideration in a framing job or when the framed piece must be shipped. Plexiglas® is a brand name of Rohm and Haas and is an acrylic sheet.

ULTRAVIOLET-FILTERING ACRYLIC

The same as acrylic sheeting mentioned above, but with the addition of UV-filtering added to the formula during manufacturing. There are many suitable types available from several manufacturers. Some types have a slight amber cast. Read the manufacturer's specifications.

Acrylics cannot be used with friable art, i.e. charcoals, pastels and pencil drawings because the static quality of the plastic will cause particles to lift off the art and adhere to the glazing.

STYRENE

This is a cheaper form of plastic that should not be used in framing. It yellows as it ages, and the yellowing is accelerated by exposure to heat and sunlight.

MAT DECORATION FOR CONSERVATION FRAMING

Although conservation framing is commonly associated with simple, spare museum-style presentation, this look is not a requirement and may not suit all customers. Many mat decoration techniques can be used to add interest and color. Use the same criteria when choosing and using materials for decoration that should be used for all conservation procedures.

SHAPES, CUTS, CARVING
Once suitable conservation boards have been selected, all sorts of creative cutting techniques can be used to dress up the matting design. Memorabilia mats and other multiple opening situations can be given visual interest with varied shapes and sizes, and inventive layouts.
V-grooves, inlays, stencils, hand-carving–any decorative cut can be a conservation framing option.

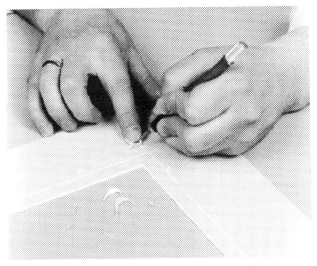

Carving into the surface of a rag matboard provides a subtle elegance for fine art.

PAINTS AND INKS
Use fine quality artist's watercolors, acrylic paints, and permanent inks. Make sure all decoration is thoroughly dry before closing in a frame.

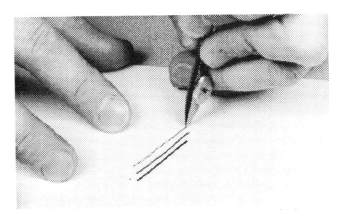

Ruling pens will carry a wide variety of paints, and inks.

FAUX FINISHES
Faux finishes include speckling, marbling, sponging–any surface decoration the frame shop offers can be used in conservation matting as well.

DECORATIVE TAPES
Since the adhesives will not be in contact with the artwork, some decorative tapes can be used on conservation mats.

Determine the composition of the materials to establish their suitability for conservation framing. Look for polyvinyl acrylic adhesive, and conservation-quality papers.

French Mats
Water color panels
Wash panels

Known by many names, soft-colored watercolor washes between India ink lines are a traditional decoration on mats

The color washes do not have to be soft–bright, primary colors give a playful accent to animation cels, and black lines in varying thicknesses can add weight and dignity to old documents. Mat bevels can also be painted providing acrylic paint is used. Artist's acrylic paint is water-based and permanent. Once dry acrylics will not harm the art.

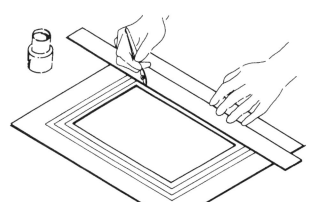

Using India ink and a ruling pen, ink the panel lines.

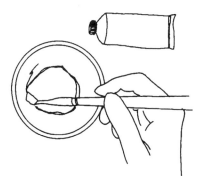

Mix fine artists quality watercolors with a little water to the consistency needed.

After the ink has thoroughly dried, lay a wash of clear water to prepare the panel for color.

Other Useful Tools & Materials

Air-Bulb
This rubber device has a bulbous end. When squeezed it blows a puff of air. It is used to blow dust and fragments of dirt from artwork surfaces. It may also be used to "suck" off particles from paper surfaces.

Blotters
These are soft, acid-free, absorbent papers, available in various thicknesses in sheets of several sizes (including large) and also in rolls. Used in many conservation techniques.

Bone Folder
This smooth, pointed bone is great for gentle smoothing and creasing. Several shapes are available.

Brushes
A collection of brushes should be set aside for conservation framing use only. For example, designate a small sable brush specifically for spreading paste onto rice paper hinges. Large, flat, soft Japanese brushes are used for spreading paste or dusting surfaces.

Canned air
Cans of pressurized air can be used to remove dust, dirt, and repair debris (such as eraser particles) from artwork surfaces. Be sure to choose a product that sprays clean, moisture-free bursts of air.

Crepe Square
This is sometimes called an "artist's pickup". This rubber-like square is good for picking up rubber cement and other rubber adhesives.

Cotton Gloves
A staple tool among conservators, white cotton gloves are very useful for many conservation framing techniques.

Deacidification Spray
Deacidification solutions consist of an acid-neutralizing agent, a liquid carrier, and a dispersant. They can be sprayed onto most kinds of paper art to neutralize the acids already present and provide an alkaline reserve against future acid attack.

Dry Cleaning Pads
These pads are filled with vinyl granules and will gently lift loose soil and dirt from a print. Brand names such as Skum-X, Opaline, Teledyne or Puffy are available.

Ethyl Alcohol
This is grain alcohol. A suitable grade is available at pharmacies. It is used in conservation procedures such as repairs.

Mylar D®
This is a strong, transparent, uncoated, untreated, acid-free polyester film. Use it for encapsulation or slipsheets. It is stable and will not deteriorate. Acetate or cellophane cannot be substituted for Mylar. Mylar is sold in sheets, rolls, and envelopes. For most art, a 3 - 5 mil. Mylar works well.

Scalpel
A couple of types and sizes of these fine, sharp blades on handles are useful for many techniques.

Spacers
Commercially-made acid-free acrylics in several different sizes and styles, usually with an acid-free adhesive side. Or use sealed balsawood strips. Spacers attach under glass, hidden in the rabbet of the frame to provide airspace between artwork and glazing.

Spatula
A small flexible spatula is useful for folding hinges, applying paste, and slitting paper.

Tweezers
A couple of different sizes and styles, such as bent-nosed and finely-pointed, will be helpful.

Water
There is much disagreement in the conservation community about which type of water is best for conservation procedures. There are disadvantages to each of the different choices: tap water, mineral water, distilled water, and deionized water. **Tap water** is usually considered unacceptable because its content of chemicals is unknown, and varies from season to season. **Mineral water** could add unwanted minerals to the paper. **Distilled water** has a neutral pH when fresh, but soon becomes slightly acidic as it dissolves carbon dioxide. **Deionized water** is so purified that it can become "ion hungry" and can leach beneficial ions, such as calcium, from the paper. Many conservators solve this dilemma by using distilled or deionized water, compensating for the deficiencies by adding small amounts (such as 2%) of calcium carbonate. The best practical choice for framers may be distilled water.

Weights
Glass paper weights or lead shot encased in double layers of smooth cotton, these are intended to hold artwork in place, when attaching hinges to backing boards. Purchase them from conservation suppliers or make them, but be sure the surface is completely non-damaging to artwork and kept clean.

CHAPTER 6

METHODS OF SUPPORTING THE ARTWORK

MATS • SUPPORTS • ENCAPSULATION • HINGES

The right support system must be strong enough to support the artwork and be completely reversible without leaving any residue or impressions on the art.

If a customer wants to remove the art from its conservation framing, whether the request comes tomorrow, next year or 10 years from now, a framer should be able to remove the art from its support without damage to the piece.

Framers may think that their shortcuts and indiscretions are safely hidden behind the dust cover; but this isn't always true. All of the auction houses, as well as astute collectors, remove the art from its frame before assessing its value.

They analyze the work's condition. If they discover that the art has been dry mounted, or if acidic tapes have been used and the art has stains, the piece is substantially devalued. It is no longer considered in mint condition.

Proper support of the art in the frame is critical. Because of the wide variety of artwork framers must handle, it is important to become familiar with a number of different support methods and materials.

The techniques in this chapter are based on the conservation rule that all materials (see Chapter 5) that touch the art are non-damaging, stable and reversible.

- An easy and safe method is to attach the work to the backing board without hinges or adhesives, using independent supports. Though this is an excellent method, it is only suitable for works that do not bend easily.

- The most frequently used support method in conservation framing is the hinge method, using acid-free, water-reversible paste and hand-made Japanese paper hinges. This time-honored technique is favored by professional conservators.

- The least-favored support material, pressure-sensitive tapes, should be used in contact with the art only in rare instances when other methods will not work.

Proper support of the art in the frame is critical. Because of the wide variety of artwork framers must handle, it is important to become familiar with a number of different support methods and materials.

Methods

A. Independent
   no adhesives

B. Hinges
   totally water reversible

C. Special Situations
   pressure-sensitive

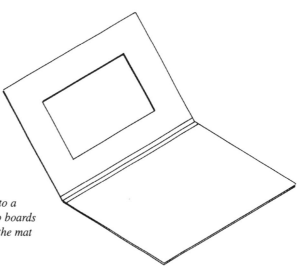

The basic mat is composed of a window mat attached to a backing board of the identical material. Attach the two boards together on the longest side -- either the left or top of the mat using pressure-sensitive linen/cotton tape.

INDEPENDENT SUPPORTS
NO ADHESIVE, NO HINGES

These methods provide support without any adhesives touching the art. This type of support is completely reversible and does not cause any damage to the artwork. Removal is simple, free of water and solvents. These factors make these techniques safe support systems.

Mounting strips and corner pockets cannot provide sufficient support for thin, flimsy materials such as Japanese papers, tissue paper or tracing papers unless there is a wide border that will be held in place by the window mat. Gravity can cause weak artwork to slump and buckle.

Encapsulation can be used on a wide variety of art: i.e. thin, weak, fragile, or brittle artwork.

MOUNTING STRIPS

ArtSavers®
Mounting troughs or flanges are commercially-prepared supports made from 1-ply Bristol board, which is scored. Leave the release paper on the tape until using the strips.

1. Position the art on the backing board.
2. Check the mat window to be sure the art is in the right position.
3. Allow ¹⁄₁₆" between the trough and the art. Peel off the adhesive and attach the trough to the backing board.
4. Generally use one trough on each side of the art. But for very large works, place the troughs at 5-6" intervals, using at least two for the bottom edge.

Lineco Mounting Strips®
A strip of 1-ply rag is faced with a piece of clear Mylar and backed with double-sided adhesive. Available in 4 inch strips as well as 12 inch and longer. These strips are very versatile and can be used with a wide variety of art work.

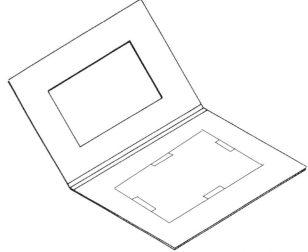

Basic placement-- use one strip on each side of the art. For very large works, place the strips at 5-6" intervals, using at least two for the bottom edge.

Pull the release paper from the back side of the ArtSaver to expose the adhesive.

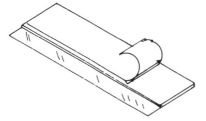

Lineco Mounting Strips

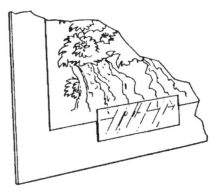

CORNER POCKETS

The principle of this method is similar to the old photo corners that were used to hold pictures into photo albums. The method is clean and simple. Make sure the corners are not attached too tightly, so that the art has room to expand and contract.

This technique does have some disadvantages. Large works tend to put too much weight on the pockets. Also when the artwork is hanging on the wall, too much of its weight is forced onto the bottom pockets. This could bend the bottom of the work or cause the art to sag.

Corner pockets may purchased, or they can be made in the frame shop using buffered paper or Mylar, scissors and a roll of acid-free (linen or paper) pressure-sensitive tape.

Position one corner mount on each corner of the artwork, allowing a slightly loose fit to accommodate expansion and contraction of the paper.

Corner pockets are available in several sizes and configurations. Some have cut-out areas for a wider viewing area.

Corner pockets are suitable for trading cards, greeting cards, reproductions, limited edition prints and some photographs.

They are not suitable for flimsy tissue-like items since the artwork will be "pinned" at the four corners, which may cause buckling or bowing. If an artwork has a large carrier (the white border around a print or reproduction) the mat that covers the carrier will add significant support to the corner pockets.

Large corner pockets with full back and cut out face.

FULL-SURROUND EDGE-STRIP SUPPORTS

This method fully encases the edges of the artwork in long paper troughs. The troughs are attached to the backing board. The artwork is gently but securely supported, with no adhesive touching the art.

1. Cut four strips of Japanese paper, the weight chosen according to the weight of the artwork the strips will support.

    Three of the strips should be about 1/2" to 1" wide, and a few inches longer than the top and side edges of the art. Fold these strips in half lengthwise.

    The fourth strip should be wider than the others, and several inches longer than the bottom edge of the artwork. Fold it lengthwise with a back that is much wider than the front. This will be the bottom trough, and its wide side will provide extra strength at the back of the art.

2. Lay the art on its backing board. Position the window mat over the art. Place a weight on the art. Remove the window mat.

3. Place the top and bottom strips on the art. Place a weight on each of these strips.

4. Lay the side strips along the side of the art, and mark the points where the top and bottom strips will intersect with these side strips.

5. Slice the folds of the side strips between the intersection points.

A full surround support permits the albumen photograph to be supported without hinges or pastes. The Archival Photomount Matboard provides the alkaline-sensitive environment required for the albumen photograph.

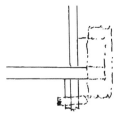

6.. Feed the top and bottom strips through the cuts in the side strips, sliding each side strip carefully into place over the side edges of the art.

7. Tape both ends of all four strips securely to the backing board.

8. The mat will cover the paper strips.

This is suitable for many paper objects that are not able to be hinged.

PAPER TRAY

This is another surround strip method, protecting and supporting the art on all four sides, and also from behind.

1. Cut a piece of acid-free paper slightly larger than the dimensions of the artwork (such as 1"-2" larger). The weight of the acid-free paper will depend on the weight of the artwork it must support.

2. Center the art face up on the paper. Make pencil marks on the paper at each corner of the art. Mark which edge is the top. Remove the art.

3. Make four straight cuts in the paper from the outer edge to the pencil marks. Cut downward from the top, and inward from the lower edge of the two sides. (See illustration.)

4. Crease and then fold the border strips created by the cuts. First fold down the top, then the two sides, then the bottom. Open folds, place artwork in "tray", and position on backing board beneath window mat. Remove window mat and mark placement of tray on backing board.

5. Remove art and secure tray to backing board using ATG strips. Place art back in tray and firmly fold edge strips, first top, then sides, then bottom. Attach tabs to backing board by taping at all four corners with linen tape.

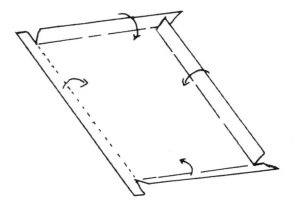

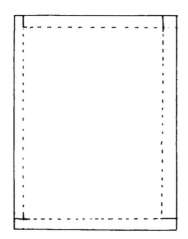

Mark placement of the art, then cut the paper from the outer edge to the pencil marks at top and sides.

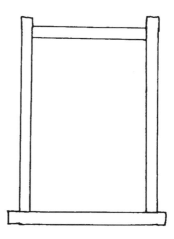

After the art has been encased in the tray, the corners may be taped to the back board.

Items suitable for encapsulation.

ENCAPSULATION

This method was developed by the Library of Congress to mount artwork without adhesives or hinges. This procedure fully encapsulates the artwork, protecting it from damage and handling.

After encapsulation the art can be matted and framed, or stored. It's a nice service to offer customers when they plan to store their work rather than frame it.

Encapsulation works particularly well for important documents that may be handled frequently, works that are too fragile to hang, or works that have been deacidified. This treatment is also good for thin paper items, newspaper clippings, diplomas, money, stamps and autographs.

Encapsulation should not be used on works that have loose media, such as charcoals, pastels and heavy graphites. The Mylar has a tendency to create static that can lift the media from the paper.

The art is encapsulated by placing it between two sheets of polyester film. It offers very good support and protection for the art.

TO ENCAPSULATE THE ART:

1. Cut two square sheets of polyester film the same size.
2. Lay one sheet on a hard, flat surface with the art beneath it.
3. Hold the art and the polyester in place using a weight in the center.
4. Apply double-stick tape to two sides and the top of the polyester, placing it 1" away from all sides of the art. The tape should be applied evenly (no gaps) and squarely at the corners.
5. On the bottom side, apply the tape, leaving an 1/8th inch gap in the corner so that air can escape. Remove the release paper from all four sides of the tape.
6. On the bottom side, just above the tape, place a 1/8th inch wide strip of Japanese paper. This will protect the

bottom of the artwork from sliding down and touching the tape.

7. Remove the weight. Carefully place the art in the center of the tape. Do not touch the art to the adhesive. Lay the second sheet of polyester over the art.
8. Carefully burnish the polyester to the tape. Trim the polyester as needed.

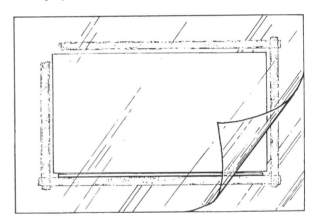

Encapsulation made with two sheets of 5 mil Mylar®, #3M 415 double sided tape, and a 1/8th inch piece of Japanese tissue.

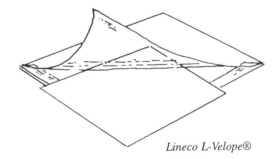

Lineco L-Velope®

DOUBLE-SIDED MAT ENCAPSULATION

This mat enables the display of artwork that has two sides. Made from two window mats that are taped together, this mat is particularly good for historical documents and letters.

Normally, one would not want to attach the artwork to a window mat; however, for this method, it is necessary to do so. Attach the artwork to the back mat.

1. Cut two window mats with appropriate openings for the artwork. Save the fallouts.

2. On the longer side, tape the boards together, using 1" wide conservation-quality tape.

3. Align the artwork with the openings. Close the mats. Double-check the positioning of the art. Replace the fallout in the back window.

4. Place the mat package on the work table, front window up. Weight the art. Carefully open the mat package

5. Hinge the art to the back window mat using a T-hinge.

If the artwork is thick, such as a booklet or magazine, it may be necessary to add support using strips of rag matboard attached to the inside of one of the mats. this would provide the booklet a "shelf" to set on.

Encapsulation can be made using Mylar®, purchased as L-Velopes® or as Showgard® envelopes available from philatelic shops that sell stamps and coins.

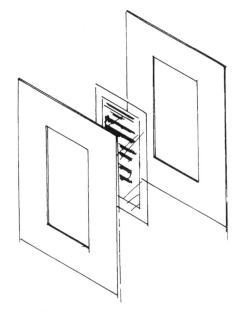

Two mats; one facing each direction.
The encapsulated art should be attached to the back mat.

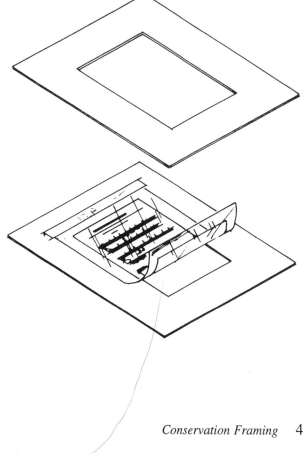

SINK MAT

The sink mat is a good way to frame something that is thicker than a regular sheet of paper, such as mounted photographs, drawings, pastels, watercolors, books, magazines, cast paper and other three-dimensional works. These items pose bulk and weight problems, making them more difficult to frame.

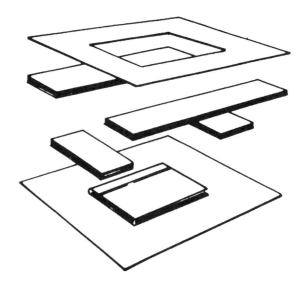

The reason this is called the "sink" mat, is that the art actually rests within a custom-made sink beneath the mat. Layers of matboard are built up along all sides of the backing board to the thickness of the art itself. This may be just one layer, or many layers as needed. Since the window mat opening is cut at least ⅛" smaller than the art, it holds the art against the backing board.

When creating this type of mat, it is important to keep in mind that all edges of the filler boards must be flush with the mat.

1. Cut the window opening so that it is ⅛" smaller than the art on each side. The mat opening will cover up ⅛" of the edge of the art.

2. Set the art in the center of the backing board. Match up the backing board, art and window mat, exactly as they should be when complete.

3. Hold the art in place with weights and set the window mat aside.

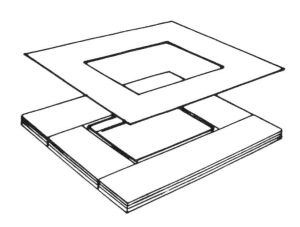

4. Approximately 1/16" away from the art, lay strips of matboard or acid-free foam center board on the backing board. Attach each layer with ATG. Build up the layers so that they reach the same height as the art.

5. Set the window mat on top and tape along the left side.

6. If additional support is needed, the art can be hinged onto the backing board. To reinforce the art, before building up the layers of board on the backing board, hinge the artwork to the backing board (see T-hinges, page 52). Allow the hinges to dry under weights before building the rest of the sink mat.

HINGES

The hinge method has long been used in museums as well as galleries. Hinges are often favored because they serve as shock absorbers, taking the force of rough handling or dropping. Hinges allow the piece to hang as well as respond to atmospheric conditions. When changes occur in the humidity and temperature surrounding the art, the art-work and framing materials react by either expanding or contracting.

The number and size of the hinges, where they should be placed and what kind of paper they are made from all depend on the size, weight, condition and use of the art.

RULES FOR USING HINGES

- Hinges should be made from Japanese papers. These papers create strong, yet flexible, thin hinges, which are reversible, non-staining and acid-free.

- The paper used for the hinge should be slightly thinner and weaker than the art.

- Artwork should be hinged from the top.

- Use the minimum number of hinges that will give sufficient support. Use enough hinges to evenly distribute the weight of the artwork without buckling.

- Do not make hinges too tight. Wrinkling or cockling can occur, or, even worse, the art may tear.

- The hinges should never be larger than what is necessary to hold the art.

- For most works, use a hinge near, but not at each of the top corners. One rule of thumb is to place hinges in from the corner of the art by a distance equal to the width of the hinge.

- Hinges should be attached with cooked rice paste, wheat starch paste or methyl cellulose paste.

- Never attach the art to the window mat. Always fasten it to the backing board. With double-sided mats, attach art to the back mat.

- Very large or heavy art may need additional support. Provide support by using extra hinges, a bottom mounting strip or a flange.

MAKING HINGES

To make Japanese paper hinges, tear the paper into small rectangular strips with delicate, soft feathered edges. The hinges are torn, never cut.

Tearing enables the long fibers to separate at their weakest point, leaving the stronger fibers intact. Also, by tearing the paper, the hinge has soft, irregular, feathered edges. These edges blend in nicely with the art, so there are no visible hinge marks from the front. Straight-cut edges have sharp ridges that can make indentations in the art.

The size of the hinge depends on the size of the art. For example, for artwork of average weight measuring 14x18" the size of the hinge should be approximately 1½" wide by ½" deep. Crosspieces for this hinge should be approximately 2" wide.

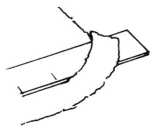

Japanese paper may be torn on the edge of a ruler.

WET CUTTING HINGES

1. Hold the paper up to the light. Since the paper is translucent, a grid of fibers can be seen in it. Some fibers are closely spaced. Perpendicular to those are widely-spaced fibers. Those are called chain lines. Using a pencil, mark the direction of the chain lines with an arrow. For maximum strength, cut all hinges parallel to chain lines.

2. Place a ruler or straightedge parallel to the chain lines to direct the tear.

3. Dip a watercolor brush or ruling pen in water, then draw it along the straightedge. Score the line with a bone folder.

4. Holding the straight edge firmly, pull gently on the paper, tearing it along the score.

5. Continue wet cutting the hinge on all four sides.

6. Attach the hinges to the art using cooked starch or methyl cellulose paste.

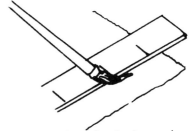

Wet-cutting requires a brush of water drawn over the area of the paper to be torn.

Holding a ruler over the wetted area and pulling the paper away from the edge will give the best feathered edge for hinge-making.

MAKING PASTE

RECIPE FOR WHEAT STARCH PASTE
Ingredients
- 1 Tablespoon Dry Starch
- 5 Tablespoons Water

Place the starch in a saucepan. Slowly pour in the water. Stir 10 - 15 seconds until the mixture is smooth. Let the starch soak for a few minutes, stirring occasionally. Warm over low heat for 5 - 10 minutes on an electric or gas range, stirring frequently.

After the mixture has warmed, increase heat to high, stirring constantly for approximately one minute or until the paste thickens and becomes gray and translucent. Continue to stir constantly another 15 - 20 minutes, until paste is batter thick. Do not boil.

A double-boiler method also works well. It will take longer to cook, but there is less risk of burning.

Allow the paste to cool, stirring frequently until room temperature or cooler. If it is necessary for it to cool quickly, set the container in cold water, stirring constantly.

After the paste has cooled, strain it through a small-meshed strainer, such as synthetic window screen stretched over a cup. Use the back of a spoon to smooth lumps. Strain again if necessary.

The paste should be the consistency of thick cream. If it becomes too thick, thin with water. Overly thick paste will make the hinges too stiff, and will create a brittle bond. Thin paste will wrinkle the artwork.

Keep paste in an air-tight container in a cool place. Do not refrigerate. The paste should last three or four days. Then, it will spoil and lose its adhesive power.

Some framers prefer to add a few drops of OPP (o-phenyl phenol) solution in ethyl alcohol to deter mold growth and extend the life of the paste. However, there is evidence that fungicide additives can cause chemical changes, activated by exposure to light, that may eventually discolor paper that is in contact with the paste.

A practical "double-boiler" for the frameshop can be made from a "Hot Pot" that boils water and a clear glass Pyrex® bowl.

The best solution to the short shelf-life of wheat starch paste is to make fresh paste frequently.

MICROWAVE METHOD
Mix starch with water in microwave-safe container. Cook on high for 20-30 seconds, then stop microwave and stir paste. Repeat several times until paste is thick, approximately 3 to 4 minutes total. Then cool and strain.

RICE STARCH RECIPE

Ingredients: 2 Tablespoons of rice starch
1 Pint water

Mix the starch with a little bit of the water, stirring to a thick cream consistency. Bring the rest of the water to a boil. Add starch mixture to boiling water, then reduce heat to bring solution below boiling point. Stir constantly over moderate heat until thick and glossy. Cool and strain.

T-HINGE

This basic hinge includes a tab which is attached to the artwork on the back upper-most area of the art and a crosspiece which holds the tab to the backing board.

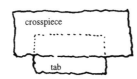

Its construction is meant to separate if the piece is shaken or dropped. The hinge will let go at the crosspiece section allowing the art and the tab-portion of the hinge to separate from the crosspiece. If the hinges are too strong the art might tear.

ATTACHING THE HINGES TO THE ART

1. Working on a blotter, use a small brush to apply a small amount of paste to the hinges. Use several strokes so that some of the paste penetrates the hinge paper. Too much adhesive will cause the hinges to buckle.

2. When the paste on the hinges is no longer shiny, meaning that excess moisture has been absorbed by the blotter, they are ready to attach to the art. Use a pair of tweezers to apply the hinge to the back of the top edge of the art. Attach them to no more than ⅛" -¼" of the art. Another suggested rule of thumb is to attach 1/3 of the hinge to the artwork, 2/3 to the backing board. Apply hinges near, but not at, the corners of the art.

3. Do not rub the hinges while they are wet, as this could stretch the fibers in the paper, causing them to buckle. Place a blotter over the hinges, and press lightly on the blotters to pick up excess dampness. To prevent cockling, change the blotter if it becomes wet. If the hinges do buckle, dampen them, and remove them immediately. Allow the art to dry before attempting another hinge.

4. Cover the blotters with a piece of glass or an acrylic sheet, held in place by weights. Let the hinges dry under pressure. Watch for creases or excess moisture in the blotters. Replace them if necessary. Drying may take from 10 - 12 minutes, but could take up to an hour, depending on the consistency of the paste. Drying is a very important step in the hinging process, because starch pastes are low-tack adhesives that bond during drying.

ATTACHING THE HINGES TO THE BACKING BOARD

Once the hinges are dry, the art can be attached to the backing board.

1. Position the image in its proper place on the backing board. Check placement of the window mat. Then use weights to hold the art in place while the hinges are attached to the backing board.

2. Apply paste to the entire surface of the crosspiece, set the crosspiece across the tab.. This creates a "T". Since this crosspiece does not touch the art, it is not necessary that it be feathered.

Note: Do not place the crosspiece next to the top of the artwork. Allow a bit of space from the top of the art to the bottom of the crosspiece.

3. Repeat the blotting and weighting process outlined in the attaching of the tab section.

Drying is a very important step in the hinging process, because starch pastes are low-tack adhesives that bond during drying.

V-HINGE

A V-hinge is used for an invisible mount. Most often it is used in float mounting, giving the art the appearance of floating within the window opening. It is suitable for small artwork because it is weaker than the other hinges.

The v-hinge is a rectangle of Japanese tissue folded upon itself and then attached to the artwork.

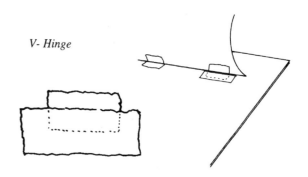

V- Hinge

1. Position the artwork in the window opening. Use a couple of small weights to hold it in place.
2. On the backing board, lightly mark the upper corners of the artwork with a pencil.
3. Carefully lift the artwork up from the bottom and turn it over, so that it is laying face down, with the top edge of the artwork resting just slightly above the marked pencil lines. Be careful not to crease or bend the art. Hold the art in place with weights.
4. Gently lift the corners of the art and erase the pencil marks.
5. Apply paste to the tab portion of the hinge and wait until the adhesive is no longer shiny with wetness. 6. Attach one end of each hinge to the artwork, allowing the remainder of each hinge to rest on the backing board. Gently dab along the full length of the hinges with a blotter, to secure them in place and absorb some of the excess moisture.
6. Place dry blotters and weights over the hinges until they are dry. When dry, crease the hinges, folding them downward so that the art is face up on the mounting board. The hinges are invisible behind the art.

7. Reinforce the hinge by adding a crosspiece. To do this, before attaching the hinge to the backing board, apply paste to the entire surface of the crosspiece. lace the hinge where desired on the backing board, and place the crosspiece over it. The top edge of the crosspiece should be away from the art. Place blotters and weights over the hinges until they are dry.

FLOAT HINGE

The pass through hinge provides a strong support. It is good for heavy artwork, such as cast paper and heavy watercolors.

1. Using Japanese paper and starch attach a small portion of a long strip of Japanese paper to the back side of the art work. Keep the attachment about 1/4" down from the top edge of the art.
   Attach as many hinges as needed. For large pieces you may need three or four.
2. Cut two horizontal slits in the backing board. Use a straight-line mat cutter to cut clean, angled slits 1/4" down from the edge of the art.
3. Pass the hinges through the slits.
4. Adjust the hinge tabs on the back of the backing board. Paste the hinges onto the back of the backing board.
5. To reinforce this hinge, use a crosspiece. Before attaching the hinge onto the back of the backing board, apply paste to the entire surface of the crosspiece. Place the hinge where desired on the reverse side of the board and place the crosspiece over it.
6. Place blotters and weights over the hinges until they are dry.

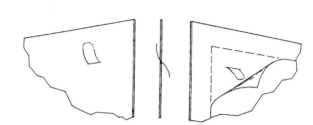

EXTRA STRENGTH HINGES

This type of float hinge is reinforced for art that is difficult to attach to due to poor condition or surface irregularities of the paper.
This hinge provides extra strength for floating heavy papers.

1. Tear a double-length hinge. Fold hinge in half, then fold the last 1/4" of each loose end outward, forming a narrow "T" shape.
2. Paste folded part of hinge along its entire length, making a double-thick hinge.
3. Paste the flat "T" portion of the hinge to the back of the artwork.
4. Mark placement of artwork, pass hinges through slits in backing board and attach to back of board as described for Float Hinge.

Profile of a float hinge with a Z hinge at the lower edge.

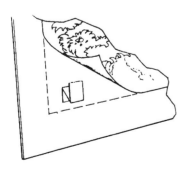

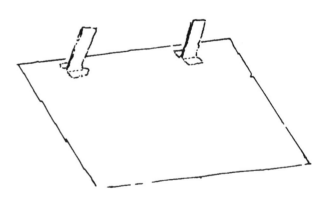

Back of artwork with two Extra Strength Hinges.

CHAPTER 7

DEACIDIFICATION

Acid in paper is the cause of 80 to 95 percent of all yellowness, embrittlement and deterioration in paper. At one time more than 16 million books in the Library of Congress, which contains the world's largest and most valuable collection of books, were considered "endangered," and were reportedly turning to dust at a rate of 200 per day. Their acidic woodpulp paper pages were rapidly self-destructing. For many years, scientists sought methods to save endangered papers. Fortunately for those books, and for all acidic papers, a safe and very effective technology has emerged--deacidification.

In 1968, Richard D. Smith, Ph.D., at the Graduate Library School of the University of Chicago, developed chemicals and techniques that neutralize paper acid and halt decay. From this early technology today's deacidification products have been refined.

Deacidification solutions consist of an acid-neutralizing agent, a liquid carrier (solvent), and a dispersant. While they don't actually remove acids, these solutions penetrate the cells of the paper and neutralize the acids already present within.

In addition, the solutions impregnate the paper with an alkaline reserve that protects the paper from future acid attacks. In fact, one application protects the art for at least 100 years.

While stopping yellowness and brittleness, deacidification also protects the work from developing brown stains that are caused by fungi. Plus, deacidified paper has added body and stability.

WHAT CAN BE DEACIDIFIED?
Deacidification has been used to preserve extremely rare and valuable documents, like three of the remaining 21 copies of the United States' Declaration of Independence, letters from Abraham Lincoln and George Washington, posters and watercolors by Toulouse-Lautrec, Audubon's four volume elephant portfolio, *Birds of America*, and etchings by Rembrandt.

Deacidification has been used on all kinds of books, documents, paper art, mounted black and white photographs, baseball cards, stamps, comic books and old newspaper clippings.

It may also be used to neutralize the backs of some paint-ings that are backed with acidic panels and thick mounting boards. In fact, practically any paper item that should be preserved and that is highly acidic (testing lower than 7 or 8 pH) can be treated.

Deacidification is easy to do, and it can be a great extra service to offer customers.

The Products
Deacidification solutions are available as aerosol sprays or as liquid solutions. Most picture framers will find the sprays easiest and most convenient to use.

WEI T'O®: This manufacturer makes two lines of products. The first line has been available for a number of years. It is offered in three formulations, and all three come in aerosol spray or liquid solutions. All use magnesium carbonate as the deacidification agent. All of the sprays use HFC-134A, a fluorocarbon, as their propellant. The different formulations are designed for use on different weights of paper and different types of artwork.

Chemically speaking, Solution #2 and spray #10 contain HCFC-141B as the solvent and methanol as co-solvent; #3 and #11 use HCFC-141B as solvent and ethanol as co-solvent; and #4 and #12 have a greater proportion of ethanol for greater penetration of paper.

Wei T'o has recently launched a new line of products called the "Good News" line, which offers a number of improvements increasing safety and ease of use. While continuing to use an organic magnesium carbonate as the deacidification agent, these sprays and solutions also contain only natural, organic solvents and propellants. The "Good News" products have little or no effect on printing inks and other art media. There are significantly less problems with feathering and bleeding. The spray valves are unlikely to clog during storage. Although all of the ingredients in the new formulas are commonly found in household products (the propellant is propane and the co-solvent is isopropyl alcohol), good ventilation practices are still important.

BOOKKEEPER®: Developed and manufactured by Preservation Technologies, Inc. for the mass deacidification of books and documents in libraries and archives, Bookkeeper products are also available to the picture framer.

The ingredients in these gentle formulas are nontoxic and nonflammable. Magnesium Oxide is the deacidification agent. Bookkeeper uses a non-solvent, environmentally friendly liquid carrier (perfluoroalkane) to disperse the magnesium oxide into the paper. It does not dissolve or change the colors of ink, dye, and most other media. Unlike water, this liquid carrier is able to "wet" the paper without swelling the fibers.

Tests show that papers treated with the Bookkeeper products typically show a pH level between 7.5 and 9.5., and meets Library of Congress standards for a permanent and stable alkaline reserve. This is especially important, because during the past couple of years the Bookkeeper Mass Deacidification facilities have been treating tens of thousands of books for the Library of Congress!

Available to picture framers in a pump bottle or aerosol can, the Bookkeeper formula does not clog spray nozzles. As with the Wei T'o products, although the formula ingredients are nontoxic, good ventilation is still important.

TESTING THE ART
Despite the gentleness of the newer formulas, all artwork MUST BE TESTED before deacidification Some papers contain heavy concentrations of lignin. While these papers need deacidification the most, the treatment solutions may darken the papers and, in turn, alter the colors in the art. Also, the colors and inks in some prints and drawings may run or blur when deacidified.

Test each color before proceeding with the deacidification treatment.

Many art papers have subtle surface characteristics that can be altered if deacidification is not evenly applied. Aerosol spraying is usually the safest and fastest method of deacidification for framers.

Also, any paper that has been repaired with tape, or is constructed in an unusual way, may absorb the solution unevenly and may create problems. Test all materials and colors in the art to be certain.

If testing the art is inconclusive, contact either a paper conservator or the manufacturer of the solutions. The old adage "better safe than sorry" really applies to working with items of value.

PERFORMING THE TESTS

Do not take chances. Always test and prove the procedure before proceeding with deacidification.

Use precautions. Even though deacidification solutions are non-toxic, they should be used in well-ventilated areas. Vapors in the workroom should not exceed OSHA limits. Material safety data sheets are available from the manufacturers.

1. Spray one teaspoon into the spray can cover cap. Or, if using a "dipping" method of deacidification, pour one teaspoon of solution into a small dish or bowl.
2. Dip a cotton swab into the solution.
3. Carefully roll the cotton swab over each different color or other media in the artwork. Test all colors, even the black lines around the work and the artist's signature.
4. Examine the treated areas and the cotton swab.
5. If no change occurs, dampen (do not soak) another cotton swab in water. Dampen and re-examine each area that was tested before. Check to see if the colors are still stable.
6. If there is any color change after either of the tests, stop and consult with the product manufacturer or a paper conservator.
7. If there is no change after these tests, proceed with the deacidification process, carefully following the manufacturer's guidelines.

SPRAYING THE ART

1. Remove any loose dust or dirt from the art by using a sable brush.

2. Place artwork face down on a spraying board (see illustration). One of these can be easily made using plastic sheeting and a furnace filter available at a hardware store.

3. Tilt actuator on the spray can, so that the spray strikes the paper at the proper angle.

4. Spray to the side of the art to clear the can's nozzle. This is a good practice even with the newer, non-clogging formulas, because a clogged nozzle could produce an uneven splatter of spray.

5. Hold the spray can approximately 6" from the artwork. Wet the back of the artwork paper thoroughly and evenly by spraying the solution side to side in an overlapping pattern.

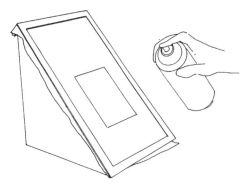

A spray booth may be made using plastic ceiling panels, and a furnace filter from the building supply store. For maximum safety, add a small exhaust fan to the back side of the booth and a dryer vent to the outside of the building.

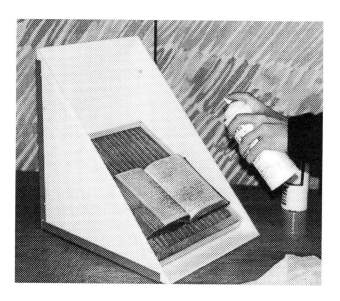

6. Now spray top to bottom in an overlapping pattern. This should entirely cover the work.

7. With older formulations, when spraying is complete, turn the can upside down, pointing the spray nozzle away, and spray until the valve is dry. This is very helpful to reduce clogging of the nozzle. If there is excessive spray build-up, use a tooth brush to clean-out the nozzle.

8. Lay the artwork flat, face down, on a protected surface, until it is dry, or dry on a suction spraying box.

9. If the artwork cockles, dry it between sheets of dry blotting paper, under moderate, even pressure.

10. To remove stains from fingers use white vinegar followed by a baking soda rinse.

CHAPTER 8

FITTING

The frame package is ready to be put together and sealed. To be properly conservation framed, everything inside the frame package must be acid-free.

The frame package will help protect the art from fluctuations in humidity. Moisture cannot enter the glass side. The filler board and dust cover hinder moisture from coming in through the back.

If it is known that the art will be placed in a humid or temperature-fluctuating environment, create an even stronger moisture barrier by sealing the back of the frame using Mylar. The frame package will not be hermetically sealed, but it will be airtight and less susceptible to temperature and humidity fluctuations.

However, if there is a change inside of the frame, it is nearly impossible for moisture to escape. It will take the internal environment a very long time to return to its original state.

The Mat Package consists of
    glazing
    the mat or spacer
    the art
    the backing board
    the filler board
    dust cover or Mylar sheet as a moisture barrier

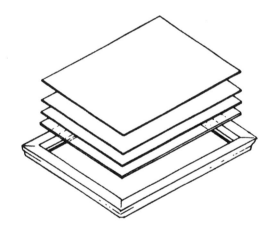

Fitting the Frame

1. Assemble all materials together on a flat, clean, dry surface. Be sure that hands are clean.

2. Clean the glazing using denatured alcohol mixed with water or a glass cleaning product from framing suppliers. The cleaner must not leave chemical residue on the glass. Do not use vinegar (which is highly acidic), ammonia or household glass cleaner that has coloring in it.

3. Use a soft brush to remove all stray lint or paper fragment from the mat package.

4. Place the frame face down. If the frame is made of wood or plastic, be sure that the inner edges are sealed, or use the sandwich fit method.

5. Sandwich fit the mat package to create an extra moisture barrier inside of the frame. Use ¾" acid-free tape, such as 3M #810 tape. Attach ⅛" of the tape to the face of the glazing, and wrap the rest of the tape around the sides of the glazing and mats. Fasten the tape to the back of the backing board. Do this on all four sides of the mat package. The taped edges of this sandwich provide a sufficient barrier to make lining of wooden frame edges unnecessary.

6. Place the mat package into the frame.

7. Place the filler board behind it.

8. Using a brad driver or point driver, secure the pieces in the frame. Do not force or pinch fit, as this could cause the art and mat to buckle.

9. Apply ATG to the back of the frame.

10. Place the dust cover on the adhesive. Use either Mylar or paper. If paper is used, pull it taut. Use a trimming knife or razor blade to cut the paper at the edge of the frame. A slight angle to the blade will create a nice, clean edge.

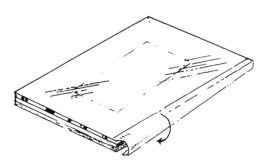

The sandwich fit:
Wrap clear tape around the edge to create a channel.
This will keep acid from wood frames from leaching
into the mat package as well as dust and particles.

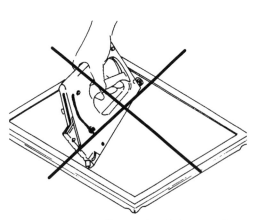

DO NOT force fit! It will create buckled mats and artwork
later on. If more space is required in a rabbet use
RabbetSpace® by FrameTek.

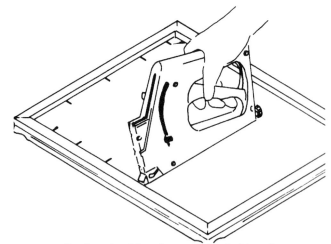

Set the point driver flat on the back side to fit
the frame properly.
Space for expansion of glazing, boards and artwork
must be permitted or buckles will occur.

11. Apply the hanging hardware. Place hardware approximately 1/3 of the way down from the top of the frame. Before inserting the screw eye into wood moulding, use an awl to poke a hole in the wood. If the moulding is hardwood, a hole must be pre-drilled with a hand or electric drill. Use fat screw eyes for soft woods and thin ones for hardwoods.

12. Choose a wire that has a breaking strength that is three times the weight of the art. Insert the wire into the screw eye twice and pull it tightly. Wrap the wire a couple of times around the screw eye. Then wrap about 1" of the excess wire onto the wire itself. Cut the wire. Do not crimp it. Do this on both sides.

13. Place bumper pads onto the bottom corners of the frame. Bumper pads stabilize the frame on the wall, provide air circulation and minimize dust collection behind the frame. The bumper pads are self-adhesive. Simply pull off the release paper and attach the pads to the bottom corners of the frame.

14. When finished, place a label on the back of the frame. The label should include the shop name, address and telephone number. An additional label may be added, stating that conservation materials and techniques were used.

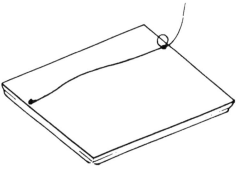

Wrap wire neatly.

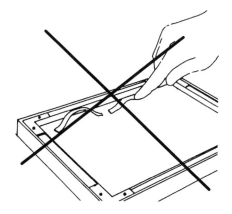

DO NOT use spring clips because they exert excessive pressure on the edges of the frame package.

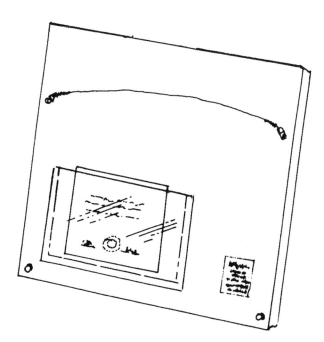

Add pockets to the back of the finished framing to hold certificates or related papers.

CHAPTER 9

HANDLING ARTWORK: SPECIAL CASES

In conservation framing, there is no such thing as "one treatment fits all artwork". Framers must tailor handling and support techniques to the type of art being framed. It is very important to be familiar with all types of art and to know as much as possible about the media, the paper, and the condition of the work.

ANIMAL SKINS

Today most papers that are called "parchment" or "vellum" are translucent commercial papers that are textured to resemble animal skins. A few universities still use parchments for their diplomas. Very old documents and diplomas are usually on real parchment.

Commercial vellum and parchment papers can be hinged in the traditional manner. However, an alternate support system may be required for animal skins because they contain oil. Because water and oil do not mix, it is difficult to attach hinges using water-based pastes or starches.

To determine if the material is parchment, moisten fingers with water (do not lick fingers) and touch a corner of the art. If it feels sticky, it is probably parchment Also, look closely at the material. Parchment and vellum are thicker than paper and they have visible pores and a skin-like look.

If the material is skin, attach the art to the backing board by using hinges made from gummed paper tape, or encapsulate it, or support it to the backing board with corner pockets or flanges.

Wrinkled Skins - Like paper, animal skins absorb moisture from the air. If the skins dry out, they will shrivel up and wrinkle. These wrinkles are normal. Except in extreme cases, they should be left alone. Unfortunately, customers often complain about the wrinkles and want them removed.

To flatten a skin document or diploma, moisture must be put back into it. Before dampening the skin, test the entire piece to be sure that the inks will not bleed. Many inks on these type of documents are not permanent.

Place the skin face down on a dry blotter paper. Over the back of the art place a blotter that has been dampened with water. Place a sheet of glass over it and allow the parchment to soak up moisture overnight. While the skin is still damp, tape it down on all four edges with linen tape to an acid-free support. Let it dry.

Framers must tailor handling and support techniques to the type of art being framed.

Once the parchment is dry, carefully remove the tape, and attach the flattened artwork to its backing board. Unlike cotton or wood based papers, which do well in an alkaline environment, animal products, like parchment and leather, actually prefer non-buffered boards.

ANIMATION CELS

One of the popular new collectibles is animation cels. Original works of art, these cels are the plastic sheets that animators actually drew and painted on. Older works are made of nitrocellulose and came from actual animation productions. Nitrocellulose wrinkles and yellows with age. It can be dangerous because it is flammable. Also, it darkens when exposed to light and frees nitric acid. Because decomposing nitrate emits fumes and resins, framed cels may need to be opened every few years to be aired out.

Newer works are generally made of cellulose acetate, and are either from actual productions or from commemorative limited editions. Some new editions are called "seri-cels", because they are actually silkscreens produced as limited edition prints.

Because the cels are very fragile, it's best to handle them a little as possible. Wear cotton gloves to avoid fingerprinting them. Do not try to clean them. Gently remove dust, fingerprints and surface soil with a clean, dry, soft cotton rag. Wipe horizontally and use very light pressure.

Animation cels, like paper, are hygroscopic and expand and contract according to the relative humidity. They should be allowed to flex just like paper art. Very dry air is dangerous to old nitrocellulose cels, and can dry them to serious brittleness in a short time.

Water-based paste will not stick to plastic, so it is not possible to attach cels to their backing boards using water-based products. Use hinges made from pressure-sensitive tape, or support the art with corner pockets or flanges.

Note that animation cel conservators prefer to mount the cels with a polyvinyl tape. They tape across the top of the cel, so that the art can swing. It is unlikely that pressure-sensitive tapes will be removable at a later date.

Use ultraviolet-filtering glazing to protect the colors and the film itself.

Framing of a cel using BriteCores ®matboard. Bugs Bunny® and Yosemite Sam® are registered to Warner Bros.

ANTIQUE PAPERS

Letters, prints, bookplates--framers encounter all manner of old papers. Antique papers may be in varying states of disrepair--yellowing, stained, brittle, torn. Deacidification will not correct deterioration, but will stop any problems being caused by acids and prevent their continuation. Mylar encapsulation can provide support for fragile papers, as can the use of multiple mounting troughs, surround support strips, and corners.

Use double-sided mats and glass on front and back to display both sides of two-sided art. Tape the mat and glass package together securely on all four sides to provide a seal since there will be no dust cover.

BARK PAINTINGS, TAPAS

Bark paintings, or tapas, are done on a paper-like material made from the inner bark of many types of plants. The stalks of the plant are cut and soaked to soften them. Then the bark is stripped, beaten and folded repeatedly until it increases to many times its original size. Large ones may be made by gluing or sewing several pieces together.

Bark paintings are often cockled and creased and they "remember" their wrinkles--they are difficult to flatten permanently. They can be fragile and brittle. The painting media can bleed, flake, and crack. Unless a bark painting is strong and sturdy, don't try to flatten it.

Most bark paintings can be hinged using Japanese papers and starch paste or methyl cellulose. The paints are often light-sensitive, so use UV-filtering glazing.

CAST PAPER

Cast paper is a three-dimensional sculpture. Essentially, it is molded, hand-made paper, and it can be heavy. A lot of collectors like to place these works in clear, Plexiglas boxes, to allow viewing from many angles. Deep shadow-box frames can also be used.

To hold the weight of the piece, it's best to use several float hinges, cutting slits in the backing board and fastening the hinges to the back side of the backing board. (see Chapter 6 "Methods of Supporting the Artwork". The pass through hinge and extra strength hinge will support paper casts.)

Antique bookplate from
Godey's Ladies Book 1864

After hinging the work, it may be necessary to add further support with a shelf made from acid-free foam center board. To make a support shelf, cut a strip of foam center board that is 12" long and 4" wide (size can be adjusted as the artwork and frame dictate.) Score the board in two places. Fold the board into a triangle. Attach the base of the triangle to the backing board using ATG. Use the edge of the triangle to support the art.

COMPUTER-GENERATED PRINTS

There are many new printing processes made possible by computers, ranging from high quality giclée prints to inkjet on canvas to simple color photocopies. The colorfast and lightfast characteristics of these various inks and techniques varies widely. Some printing methods are waxed-based, and some are printed with a thermographic process, both of which will melt. Avoid applying heat to them, or using any mounting method, including wet methods, on computer-printed papers. Use UV-filtering glazing.

DETERIORATING MATBOARDS

Generally, when reframing a customer's artwork, throw away old matboards and matting materials. However, the customer may ask to save a special French mat or hand-painted mat that may have historical or sentimental value. If forced to use acidic mats in a conservation framing situation, do as much as possible to protect the artwork from the acids.

First deacidify the old mat. Then use a 4-ply conservation matboard below the acid mat, to protect the art. Make sure this barrier mat extends at least 1/4" beyond the bevel of the old mat. The bevel may be reversed so that it is less noticeable. Do not use a barrier mat that is thinner than 4-ply. Otherwise, acids from the old board can migrate through the new matboard and onto the art.

DIMENSIONAL COLLAGE

This is a low-relief work made up of pieces of paper, cloth or other material pasted onto a canvas or board. This art form began with the Cubists, who would stick newspaper clippings to their paintings. Matisse, in his later years, made cut-out collages.

Collages that are varnished do not have to be placed under glass and can be framed like oil paintings. Those that are not varnished should be handled like paper art, hinged within a window mat or placed in a sink mat. Often collages are made with short-lived glues or incompatible

Paper and bead collage by Betty Kylin

media. Check for loose pieces that are just about to fall off, and ask customers if they would like you to reattach those that fall during framing or save them separately to be returned to the customer.

GICLÉE PRINTS

Giclée, from the French word meaning "squirt" or "spurt", is an appropriate name for this highly sophisticated inkjet printing method. These prints are also called Iris pints, named after Iris Graphics, a major supplier of these special printers. Artwork is digitally scanned, manipulated by the artist and/or printer, and stored on disk. The disk is then used to print images in small editions, in quantity, or even one at a time. The specialized printer can handle several sizes, types, and weights of paper. During printing, microscopic drops of ink are sprayed onto the substrate at a rate of millions per second, creating beautiful colors and high resolution. The prints are then sprayed with a protective coating to shield the water-based inks from smearing.

Some collectors and dealers are concerned about how edition sizes of giclée prints can be controlled. Of more concern to framers is the colorfast and lightfast qualities of the inks. So far, giclée inks have not shown good longevity. Although this problem is definitely a high priority among giclée printers, and solutions (including UV-filtering in the protective coating spray) are being worked on, for the time being UV-filtering glass and limited light exposure are suggested with giclée prints.

MEMORABILIA

Autographs, baseball cards, postcards, wine labels–many kinds of paper items become collectibles. Encapsulate thin or fragile pieces and/or use independent support methods. Conservation framing does not have to be boring. If customers want an interesting presentation for their memorabilia, be creative with arrangements and shapes of multiple opening mats, use decorative cuts and splices, etc.

NEWSPAPER CLIPPINGS

Newsprint is a cheap, disposable paper that is full of lignins; designed to have a very short life. Ultraviolet light, heat, humidity and airborne pollutants react with the inherent acids, making the paper so brittle that it virtually disintegrates in a short period of time.

Of concern to framers is the colorfast and lightfast qualities of the inks.

Newsprint is a cheap, disposable paper that is full of lignins, designed to have a very short life.

Unless the clipping is going into low-temperature storage and will not be handled, the only way to preserve it is to deacidify it. Before deacidifying any papers, be sure to test the paper and the inks. See Chapter 7.

After treatment, if the clipping is fragile or if it will be handled frequently, it should be encapsulated. See Chapter 6. Once it is deacidified and encapsulated, little harm will come to it.

An effective and popular treatment in framing is to mount newspaper clippings. Although this is not a conservation technique in the strictest sense, it may be the only practical way to preserve a clipping that is falling to pieces. Use an acrylic cold mount film such as Perfect Mount Film and mount the clipping to a gray or black conservation matboard. Dark-colored matboard keeps the inks from the back side of the clipping from showing through. After mounting, encapsulate the clipping. Due to the dry and brittle nature of the newsprint and the permanent nature of the adhesive, the clipping may never be removed from the mount.

OVERSIZED POSTERS
Very large 19th and early 20th century posters are very collectable, yet pose framing and storage problems. Their size not only makes them cumbersome to work with, but makes them more vulnerable to damage. Many were printed on a construction-type of paper and now are acidic and brittle.

Dealers who specialize in "antique" posters often have them deacidified and backed with muslin or linen. Although mounting original art is not classic conservation treatment, it has become the standard handling technique among the experts who buy and sell these posters. The fabric should be attached to the posters using a water-reversible adhesive, such as starch paste or methyl cellulose.

These posters may be dry mounted using a neutral pH tissue with a cotton backing. Available from several mounting tissue companies, this tissue was designed for papers, such as maps, that need to be handled The posters may be stretched over sealed wood bars, using a mat or spacer or a fabric covered sealed wood liner to keep the poster away from the glass. Full mounting a poster is not considered conservation framing.

PASTELS

CHALK PASTELS

These works are sometimes called paintings, even though they are created with dry chalk sticks. Since the powders have little adhesive power, the artist may stabilize the work with a fixative spray. However, many artists do not like to use the spray because it can alter the colors in their work, and may discolor over time. Sprays are not removable! They are made of lacquer, or plastics. If the artist requests that the framer spray fixes the artwork, be certain that the product used has the approval of the artist.
This is not a conservation procedure.

The problem is accentuated when the work is placed near plexiglas, acrylic, polyester or Mylar. Like a magnet, static electricity from these materials pulls particles off of the paper. Use a spacer or double mats and glass.

These paintings are very fragile. Be careful not to shake or jar them during fitting. Otherwise, flakes of the powders will be loose inside of the frame package.

This 70 year old pastel was done on a board which has now become brittle. The back side of the board was treated with deacidification spray. Then a sink mat was made to hold the piece and a mat was set over the entire piece holding the pastel in place and away from the glass.

PASTELS ON PAPER

Hinge the pastel to a backing board and double mat or use extra thick matboard, such as 6- or 8-ply, to provide sufficient space to prevent the glazing from coming into contact with the artwork.

The media will continue to flake off over time, drifting downward. Build a "trough" inside of the matboard that will disguise these loose particles. To do this, cut two window mats. The margin on the top mat should be slightly larger than the margin for the second mat. Instead of protruding beyond the edges of the top mat, the under-mat should be recessed slightly, lifting the top mat away from the surface of the artwork, and creating a channel to catch excess pastel dust.

ON BOARD OR CANVAS

Place the art in a sink mat. Then mat as usual. As the chalk falls off, it will fall into the bottom of the sink and will be less noticeable.

OIL PASTELS

Generally these paintings are done on a flimsy canvas-like paper. The easiest and best way to frame them is to hinge, mat and glass them. Care must be taken to avoid smearing the surface during handling. Some customers confuse these works with oil paintings and want them framed without glazing. For such customers, wet mount the work to a board, using a reversible adhesive such as starch or methyl cellulose paste, and frame it without glass. Make sure the customer knows the exposed surface is vulnerable to smearing.

PEN AND INK DRAWINGS

These artworks are usually done with India inks and are typically water-resistant when dry. The artist may wash a color over the entire drawing after the inks have set.

Washes of ink and watercolor may have expanded and buckled the paper. Do not try to flatten pen and ink drawings. Often, the washes are water soluble, and the work tends to pleat when attempting to flatten it. Try to explain to the customer that slight cockling is part of the beauty of original art.

Pen and ink drawings should be treated like other original paper art, hinged with starch paste to a backing board.

A pen & ink drawing on bristol board by Alice Marvin.

PHOTOGRAPHS

In general, fine art photographs should be treated like other works of art on paper.

However, special consideration must be given to matboards. Though an alkaline reserve is beneficial for nearly all paper artwork, research shows that may be harmful for many photographs, including chromogenic prints (i.e., Ektacolor®, Kodacolor® and Fujicolor®), dye transfer prints and many prints made prior to 1905.

Framers should use a good reference guide to help them recognize the various kinds of photographs. *Framing Photography Volume 6* of the *Library of Professional Picture Framing* by Allan R. Lamb is an excellent and thorough reference book.

A good matboard for photographs should be pure, free of metals, especially iron and copper, free of other photographically-active materials, such as halides and reducible sulfur, and free of buffers. Crescent Cardboard,

Inc. has made such a rag board for the photo industry, called Archival Photomount Board. It is solid cotton, naturally acid-free and does not have any buffering agents. Only the backing board and the mat that actually touches the photograph need to be non-buffered. Buffering agents from other boards in the frame package will not migrate to the photograph.

Many photographers today print their works onto photographic paper that has very wide margins. This provides space for the photographer to sign and number the work. It also enables the framer to easily hinge the photograph.

Though hinging to the backing board is the way conservators would want the photograph supported, many photographers prefer to dry mount them onto a firm support. Dry mounting involves placing a thin sheet of heat sensitive adhesive tissue between the photograph and the backing board. Practice before heat mounting photographs.

Although dry mounting is not a conservation method, it is a popular method of mounting photographs. Absolute flatness can be achieved with dry mounting. That alone appeals to many photographers and many customers as well. Flatness decreases surface imperfections and gives the photograph an illusion of greater depth.

Despite these advantages, dry mounting is not used by curators, conservators and knowledgeable collectors. It is a permanent mount and is nearly impossible to reverse without damaging the photograph. In addition, many things can go wrong in a dry mount that can damage the art beyond repair.

Some conservators worry that chemicals within the mounting tissue may eventually produce stains on the photographs. However, there is no conclusive evidence as yet that proves the tissues cause staining.

Considering all this, think carefully before dry mounting customers' photographs. Better choices are acid-free corners, flanges, mounting strips, hinges with water-based starch or, if the photograph is made of plastic, gummed paper or gummed linen tapes, or pressure-sensitive tapes. If nothing else will work, or if the customer insists on dry mounting, use caution. It may be best to have the customer sign a disclaimer.

A sepia photograph by Patricia D. Jolly.

RULES FOR WORKING WITH PHOTOGRAPHS
- Work in a clean, particle-free area.
- Have clean hands. Be careful not to touch skin, face or anything oily Photographs fingerprint very easily.
- The photograph must be spaced away from the glazing with spacers or mats.
- Use thicker double matting for large photographs to keep them from bowing forward toward the glass.
- Do not put a photograph into a polyester folder without a slip sheet over the face to protect the emulsion.

Completely read the directions on the mounting products being used. If using a heat press, keep the temperature under 180°F. Many of today's prints are on plastic papers, and they will melt at a higher temperature.

Over the years, photograph supports have included metal, glass, plastic, paper, and even leather, cloth and wood. Framing these unique photographs will require the information in Allan Lamb's book *Framing Photography*.

Ilfochrome Classics® (Cibachrome®) Prints – These prints are on a plastic support and have brilliant color and shine. A silver dye bleach process gives the color more vibrancy than regular color prints. These prints also resist fading. The surface layer is extremely fragile; it scratches and fingerprints easily. Never try to clean these prints. Try to remove surface dust with an air bulb, but never touch a brush to the surface. Try to handle Cibachrome prints as little as possible and use gloves when handling.

Because these prints are very slick, they are very difficult, to dry mount. The print mimics the surface of anything is comes in contact with, picking up every slight texture and indentation on the backing board, dry mount press and slip sheet. The surface finish can be damaged by excess heat.

Ilfochrome Classics (Cibachromes), especially large ones, tend to bulge in the center.. If the print is a fine art photograph it should be hinged using gummed paper or gummed linen tape.

Cleaning of Photographs – Use canned air, an air bulb or the softest sable brush. Any other cleaning methods can harm the delicate surface layer of most prints. Most photographic cleaning treatments have to be done by a conservator or photograph specialist.

Mounted Photographs – Many photographers make it standard procedure to dry mount their photographs to a firm support. It may be necessary to place these photographs in a sink mat.

Photographs on Canvas –These photos may be lacquered and mounted on a canvas. They can be framed like oil paintings, without glazing.

Resin-Coated Prints – These prints (often referred to as RC papers), resist moisture changes because both sides of the paper are covered in plastic. The RC print will resist water-based adhesives typically used to attach paper hinges. Support the art onto the backing board by using corner mounts, mountings strips or flanges. Or hinge it to the backing board by using gummed paper hinges or Filmoplast P-90.

If an RC print is to be dry mounted, use a suitable mounting tissue such as Seal ColorMount®. This is made specifically for RC photographs. The tissue allows air to flow through it, preventing moisture from becoming trapped between the photograph and the backing board. This tissue bonds at a temperature below 180°F.

VINTAGE PHOTOGRAPHS
Photographs from the 19th and early 20th century require special care and treatment. For vintage photographs, choose a matboard that is neutral pH or slightly alkaline, but not buffered. It also needs to be free of sulfur and peroxide, which can tarnish the silver image. Reference Allan Lamb's *Framing Photography Vol. 6* book for detailed framing techniques or practices.

PUZZLE

Limited edition or collectable puzzles can be put into a sink mat. Attach a sheet of Mylar to the underside of the window mat or the top of the sink mat with double-sided tape. The mat against the glazing will keep the puzzle in place.

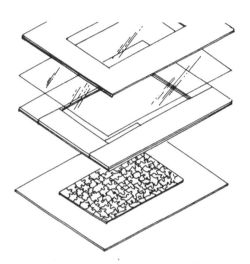

STAMPS

Stamps are popular objects to frame. Many are beautiful works of art, and are sold in "suitable for framing" presentations. There are stamp/print limited editions and often a customer wants to frame a stamp in combination with its matching print. Occasionally a customer may wish to display a full set of stamps.

To separate stamps they must be carefully folded and torn rather than cut. Single stamps and plate sets can be slipped into premade Showgard® stamp sleeves which may be purchased at a stamp store. These sleeves will encapsulate the stamps while allowing them to be floated in a frame package. The back side of the sleeves have a wettable adhesive that may be used to attach the sleeve to a backing board. A sleeve may also be created from Mylar.

Do not purchase plastic folders from an office supplier or a stationery store. Use only folders that are available from reputable stamp stores or conservation suppliers.

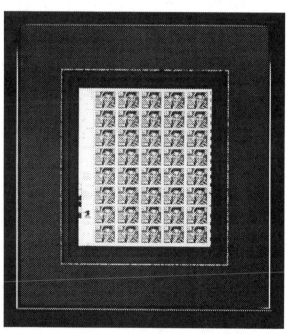

John Ranes II, CPF, GCF. framed a sheet of stamps using a Showgard mount to float them onto black blackcore matboard.

CURRENCY

Hinges may *not* be used on currency. Use a double-sided Mylar encapsulation to hold it into a mat. See Chapter 6.

WATERCOLORS

Watercolors are original works of art and should be treated in the regular conservation manner.

Light is one of the great threats to watercolors. Many beautiful works have been ruined by excessive light, heat and humidity. If the colors fade or bleach unevenly, the image will be severely distorted. Thus, ultraviolet filtering glazing is recommended.

BUCKLING – Some watercolors have been done on light-weight papers that have not been stretched and they buckle or wrinkle. The area where the artist has painted expands at a different rate than the areas where he hasn't. To prevent this, artists should stretch their papers to their maximum size before painting on them. Unfortunately, they usually do not stretch the papers.

If the customer insists on having it flat, dry mount or wet mount it to a rag board. This should only be done as a last resort, after all other alternatives have been exhausted and the customer's permission has been obtained. **Permanent mounting will greatly devalue the watercolor**. Plus, a buckled watercolor has a tendency to pleat during mounting inside of the dry mount press, folding onto itself.

When framing a buckled watercolor, be sure to allow extra space between the art and the glass. Otherwise the art may bow out and touch the glass. To create extra depth, use extra thicknesses of matboard or spacers in the rabbet of the moulding.

ON THICK PAPER – Thick paper is the popular standard for most watercolorists. There is less chance of the artist's work buckling if he uses 250 to 500 lb. paper. These papers are so thick that they usually do not need to be stretched. Most watercolor papers can be hinged to the backing board. Thicker papers, such as 500 lb., may need to be placed in a sink mat.

ON WATERCOLOR BOARD - These watercolors are done on 100lb. paper that is commercially mounted to a board. This gives the artist a stiff surface upon which to paint, and it also prevents the artwork from buckling. It may be best to place these works in a sink mat. This will provide a sturdy, stable mount, plus give the extra depth needed.

Watercolor by Patricia D. Jolly

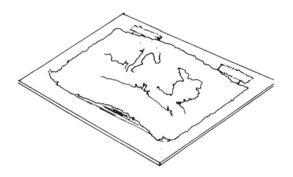

Watercolors buckle if they have not been properly prepared by the artist.

ON THIN OR JAPANESE PAPERS - Hinge these delicate paintings with Japanese papers and cooked starch paste or methyl cellulose. Since the art is thin, be sure that the adhesive is not too thick. After applying the hinge, place a dry blotter over it and weight it overnight or until it dries. This will prevent the hinges from cockling.

CHAPTER 10

PROBLEMS & SOLUTIONS

Since paper is fragile, many works of art on paper are crumpled, dented and/or torn during their lifetimes. Their surfaces become dingy and dusty. They develop stains, mildew, insect holes and scratches.

A nice mat and frame will improve the look of these works and framing can conceal damage that may be on the edges of the design area; but sometimes the damage is so obvious that it is difficult, if not impossible, to fully enjoy the art.

The rule of thumb in conservation framing is "less is best". Paper art can be ruined by hasty, injudicious amateur repairs. If the customer can be persuaded to live with the piece "as is", then leave it alone. If the damage is extensive and the work is valuable, by all means seek a conservator. *In fact, all problems with valuable works should be handled by a conservator.*

When customers insist that they want the framer to try some sort of repair, decide whether it is worth the risk and investment of time. Conservation first-aid is usually labor intensive, and some techniques require using toxic, flammable chemicals. Make sure the customer understands what you plan to do, and explain the possible consequences. A signed release form is essential before any alteration of valuable art.

The following methods are some relatively small but significant tasks that framers can usually perform without the help of a conservator. <u>Remember, all repair work is very risky, and there are no guarantees that any of these solutions will work on any particular piece of artwork.</u> Before embarking on any of these procedures thoroughly test the artwork. Many works will bleed, stain or spot. Practice all procedures on sample, inexpensive works in the shop before attempting them on the customers' works.

DRY METHOD FOR FLATTENING ROLLED-UP PRINTS
Though signed and numbered prints should be shipped and stored flat, many publishers, artists and collectors store them in poster tubes. The cost of shipping and the risk of damage are greater with flat art than art in a tube.

Remove the print from the poster tube as soon as possible. Place it face down on a clean, dry surface overnight. If this does not sufficiently relax the paper, turn the print face up, and cover with several sheets of rag board to press it flat.

*The rule of thumb
in conservation framing
is "less is best".*

*All problems with
valuable works of art
or collectibles
should be handled
by a professional
conservator.*

For added weight, place a sheet of glass on top of the mat-board. Do not lay the glass directly on the print. Leave the print like this for two or three days.

If the print does not flatten under weights and pressure, and if it is not valuable nor made of animal skins, place it on low heat in the heat press for a few minutes. Let it cool under a couple of sheets of matboard.

DAMPENING PROCEDURES

Great care should be taken when employing this method. Lightly dampen a piece of rag matboard using a sponge and water

1. Set the artwork on the board back side to the damp-ened board. Set another rag matboard on the face of the artwork.

2. Set in a warm(125 degrees) drymount press for 15 minutes then set a lite of glass on the layers of boards. Allow to set for several hours. Watch carefully.

3. The art must be thoroughly dry before putting back into a frame package. Be careful! Be sure not to flat-ten any part of the art that is supposed to be raised or embossed.

REPAIRING TEARS AND HOLES

Repairing is an area of debate among today's conservators. Contemporary conservators believe that unless the damage truly prevents the enjoyment or understanding of the work, it should be left alone – torn edges, holes and all.

Traditional conservators believe that torn art should be repaired to prevent further damage from occurring. For instance, a small tear may catch on something creating a large tear or ripping off a corner. In any case, if the art-work has a serious tear that might call for a repair, discuss this with the customer. Second, present the options to the customer, and ask her how she would like it handled.

Torn art can be repaired and weak areas can be reinforced by using a wet method. Strips of strong, thin, acid-free paper can be applied to the damaged area with reversible, colorless acid-neutral adhesive.

Repairs of valuable art are best handled by conservators

Repairs of valuable art are best handled by conservators. Framers who decide to do repairs, with the permission of the owner, should use only the papers, materials and techniques listed here. These are approved by conservators.

APPROVED PAPERS

Try to match the weight of the mending paper to the artwork. The paper must be no heavier than the art. Purchase paper from a conservation framing supplier.

- Mulberry paper
- Tengujo or Tosa – for delicate artwork or documents
- Handmade Japanese paper. Do not use machine-made Japanese papers.

ADHESIVES

Use only starch paste or methyl cellulose as adhesive. Do not use wallpaper paste, white glues, pressure-sensitive or self-adhering tapes, gummed tapes, or any non-conservation adhesive.

PROCEDURE

1. Place the art face down on a blotter on a clean, smooth, hard-surfaced area.

2. Lightly brush away any loose dirt on the torn area with a soft, sable brush.

3. Wet-tear a piece of paper to the size that will be needed. The piece should be no longer than 2" and as wide as the tear requires. If necessary, use multiple strips end-to-end to repair damaged areas that are longer than 2". The edges should be frayed and feathery, so the patch does not create a ridge on the art.

4. Place the patch on a blotter and apply paste. Be sure the paste is not too thin and watery, to prevent water from seeping onto the art.

5. Use tweezers to lift the patch strips.

6. Holding the art steady with one hand, apply the patch to the torn areas. Check to be sure the patch is placed correctly.

7. Using silicone coated release paper, pat the patch into place. Gently burnish the patch to secure adhesion. If you push too hard, the wet paper may wrinkle or split.

8. Discard the silicone paper and replace with blotting paper. Place blotting paper under the patched area.

9. To ensure good adhesion and to prevent the patched area from buckling, cover the area with a sheet of glass and weight for one hour.

10. For faster drying, lay a heavy blotter over the mend. Iron with a warm tacking iron until dry. Weight the patched area for a few minutes to prevent buckling or curling. Do not allow the tacking iron to touch the art.

Try to match the weight of the mending paper to the artwork. The paper must be no heavier than the art.

PROCEDURES FOR SPECIAL MENDING

TORN, DIRTY EDGES
Use this procedure only on margin tears. Never perform this procedure on torn design or image areas. Lay the art face down on a sheet of Mylar. Using a scalpel, lightly clean and fray fibers of the edge tears. Repeat with each edge tear. Turn the art over and repeat on the front side. Turn the art back over, so that it is face down, and repair tears with patches made from Japanese papers and starch paste or methyl cellulose paste.

TONING A DRIED MEND
A patched hole or tear may show on the face of the artwork as a bright, jagged line. Sometimes a customer will prefer that the mend be colored to soften that look. Since this is an alteration of the original artwork, and may involve the design area, it is not a conservation procedure.

If a customer insists that it be done, get a signed release stating that the customer has specifically requested and authorized the framer to do it. Mix powdered pastels, using appropriate colors. Roll a cotton swab in the pastels, dabbing tiny amounts to the front side of the patch. Use a clean swab to blend in the pastels. Use only the finest quality pastels. Do not spray with fixative.

REPAIR KITS
There are kits available for conservation mending of paper. Carefully examine each product in the kit to determine the suitability of each item for conservation purposes.

INSTA-MEND MENDING TISSUE KIT
This kit contains a 12" x 18" sheet of very fine mending tissue, four pieces of blotting paper and three pieces of nylon mesh, plus complete instructions. The conservation tissue is pre-coated on both sides with a pH neutral, water-reversible starch adhesive.

LION ARCHIVAL AALPHA TISSUE
This kit comes from Lion Archival in England. The kit contains strips of tissue, a spatula, a polyester square, a black card, a Polythene mat, a bottle of adhesive activating solution and instructions. The repair tissue is a thin alpha-cellulose material, which is coated with an acrylic adhesive. The adhesive is not tacky, but becomes tacky for about 45 seconds when the solvent is applied to it, allowing time for attachment to the paper.

The solvent evaporates quickly. For reversal, the solvent also removes the adhesive. As with other solvents, test the solution on inks, dyes and printed matter before using this product. The solution tends to effect ballpoint and felt-tip pen inks, typewriter ink and gamboge yellow watercolor.

REPAIRING TEARS WITH HEAT-SET TISSUE
Heat-setting is an alternative method to use when repairing art. The advantages are: it is fast, and it does not require weighting the patch, like wet methods. Plus, it does not risk exposing the art to water or buckling the paper.

The disadvantages are: the tissue is more expensive than Japanese papers and the patches are not as strong. They do not adhere as well as the Japanese papers.

Make sure the adhesive in the tissue is acid-free, non-yellowing, and can be reversed by reapplying heat. Many heat-set tissues are made with a release-paper backing.

1. Place the art face down on blotting paper.

2. Tear the heat-set tissue into 1/4" wide strips. Larger patches may be used for weak areas.

3. Place the tissue, shiny side down, on the tear.

4. Place a piece of silicone release paper over the tissue, if it is not already backed by silicone.

5. Heat the tacking iron to 180°F.

6. Press the tacking iron on the patch area, over the silicone paper, for several seconds, or the amount of time suggested by the manufacturer. Turn the art over and place silicone paper over the front side of the patch. Press with tacking iron for same number of seconds used on the back side of the art. Never touch the tacking iron directly to the art.

7. Peel away the backing paper or silicone paper of the patch.

Removing Surface Dirt

Removing dirt is usually a job for experts. Surface cleaning alters the surface of the paper and may cause abrasions to the paper's fibers. Do not attempt to clean valuable artworks. Send them to a conservator. In the case of photographs, cleaning is nearly always a job for a photographic conservator.

However, sometimes paper art has dirty fingerprints, fly specks or a small amount of dirt on it, that a framer may choose to attempt to remove. Use extreme caution. Always test the chosen cleaning method on the paper and the media in inconspicuous areas before proceeding.

Surface cleaning is done before any wet cleaning or mending. This prevents the dirt from permanently setting into the paper.

Always begin with the most gentle, least intrusive techniques, and test each new method attempted.

Procedures for Surface Cleaning

1. Cover the work area with a soft paper, such as blotting or kraft paper.

2. Thoroughly wash and dry hands.

3. Begin with the method that causes the least amount of stress to the art. First, try to blow off the dirt with an air bulb. Squeeze the bulb to release a jet of air. Continue until no more dirt can be removed in this manner. Blow away any dirt or crumbs.

4. If dirt remains, gently brush the area with a soft, sable brush.

5. Next, try the gentlest eraser available. Use vinyl granules or ground eraser that is neutral in color. Colored erasers can stain the paper. Some granular erasers come in cans and others come in "dry cleaning pads". Take the granules out of the pads. The pad can catch on and tear the artwork. Also, the pad becomes soiled quickly and could mark artwork.

6. Pour some granules in a spot near the artwork (not on it). Using fingertips, pick up a small amount of the granules.

Be very careful when using erasers. Artgum® will do the least damage. White vinyl erasers will remove varnish coating on process paper.

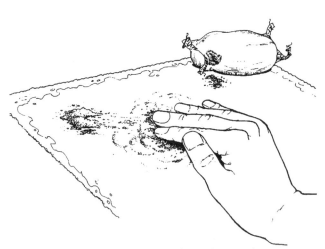

Cut the sack open to release the granules. Start in one corner and work your way over the artwork watching for color lift.

7. Roll the granules over the soiled area of the paper. Keep the paper steady with one hand. Work from the middle using small, circular strokes. Use only light pressure. Never press hard. Never use circular strokes on edges or tears. Use caution on the edges, *brush out* from the center.

8. Avoid pigmented or dubious areas. If the cleaning granules pick up color, stop immediately. Be careful not to erase valuable pencil notations made by the artist.

9. If the surface of the paper is soiled and dusty, the powdered eraser will turn dark. That means that it is picking up soil. When the granules are gray or dark, brush them away. Keep the surface area free of crumbs. The crumbs can tear or imprint the artwork.

10. Repeat the cleaning process until the crumbs no longer change color.

11. If there is an area of the art that resists the powdered eraser, a slightly stronger method may be tried, such as a vinyl block eraser. Again, test this on an inconspicuous area first.

12. Be sure that the art is weighted and remains stationary. With the eraser, stroke out from the center area. Avoid pigmented and fragile areas.

13. A narrow-tipped vinyl eraser makes it easier to get close to pigmented areas, while avoiding the image itself.

14. Strongly attached crusty material, such as fly specks or dirt spots, may be removed using a needle or a sharp scalpel. Use a flicking motion, being careful not to disturb the surface of the paper beneath it. Be careful not to pierce the paper.

15. After cleaning the surface of the art, there may still be traces of dirt on it. At this point, it may be best to leave the spots as is, rather than to risk damage by over-cleaning.

Do not try to clean art made with loose pigments, such as charcoals, pastels, chalks, pencils and some watercolors.

A MULTITUDE OF WARNINGS

- Do not try to remove deep stains.

- Do not try to clean grease spots. Common cleaning products will leave residue along with a new spot.

- Do not try to repair extensive insect damage.

- Do not use any of the dry surface cleaning methods on artworks that have loose pigments, such as charcoals, pastels, chalks, pencils and some watercolors.

- Do not use these methods on book bindings, book edges, raised prints or etchings and long-fibered, Japanese papers.

- Do not use these methods on fragile works that are difficult to handle.

- For art on coated papers, use only an air bulb or a sable brush. Erasers will damage the surface of the paper.

- If erasing on slick papers, use only an art gum eraser. Other erasers will mar the gloss.

OLD JAPANESE PAPER HINGES

When reframing artwork that has been supported with Japanese paper hinges, conservators believe it's best to leave the hinges attached to the artwork. Unless the framer knows exactly what adhesive was used to attach the hinges, there is no way to know if the adhesive is water-reversible or if it requires a special solvent.

Release the artwork from the old backing board by cutting the connecting area of the hinge, between the art and the backing board. Once released, trim the rest of the hinges close to the art. Attach the new hinges next to, but not over, the old hinges. Note on the customer's work order that the art was previously attached with hinges, and since it is not known what adhesive was used, they remain attached to the art.

Removal of Newly Applied Hinges

To remove hinges that have just been applied using water-based adhesives:

1. *Cut a piece of cellulose sponge the same size as the hinge. Dampen the sponge.*

2. *Set the sponge on the hinge. Watch closely.*

3. *When the hinge shows signs of wetness, lift with the spatula.*

4. *Repeat process until the hinge has been lifted. Have patience, it takes time.*

REMOVING OLD TAPES

Most tapes are made in four layers; but only two concern the framer: the top layer, or carrier, and the bottom adhesive layer.

A good example of the "carrier" is the shiny cellophane on "Scotch Tape". Though the carrier layer is often easy to remove, it is the gooey adhesive layer that poses problems. Removing old tapes is generally a two-step process: First remove the carrier, then remove the adhesive.

CARRIER REMOVAL

Working on a flat, hard surface, remove the carrier layer with a microspatula or scalpel. Keep the blade parallel to the tape. Gently work the edge of the blade under the carrier, working along slowly. Use a slight wiggling motion.

SOLVENT REMOVAL OF ADHESIVE

Removing old adhesives with solvents is tricky. Because many of the solvents for tapes and adhesives are toxic, read and follow the directions on the solvents carefully. Provide adequate ventilation in the work area.

Always test the paper and the media (see below) before using the solvent. If the art can tolerate the solvent, paint the solvent under the taped area. The solvent should soak into the paper, making the adhesive swell. Now carefully pull off the carrier with a pair of tweezers.

TESTING THE ART

It is imperative to test the art before attempting to use solvents. Many papers have dyes, sizes and fillers that may float or move around when they come into contact with solvents.

The test is a two-part process:testing the paper, then the media. First, test the solvent on a non-image area of the work.
1. Choose the solvent.
2. Place a small drop on an inconspicuous, non-image area.
3. Blot carefully.
4. Let the area air dry.
5. Check both sides of the paper.
6. If there is no change in the paper, apply a larger amount of solvent to the same area.
7. Let air dry again.
8. Examine the front and the back of the paper again.

9.   Repeat this process until certain that the solvent being used will not harm the paper.

Once it is certain that the solvent is safe to use on the paper, test the media. Repeat the test several times in the same area.

1.   Choose the solvent.
2.   Place a small drop onto the pigment or ink.
3.   Blot with either the edge or surface of a blotter.
4.   Examine the blotter.
5.   Look at the media in the front and back. Check for sinking, feathering or bleeding.
6.   Air dry.
7.   When dry, check again. The media may have originally appeared stable, but may move as it dries.
8.   Repeat the test until certain that the solvent will not harm the media. Even though the solvent may not have affected the media during the first or second test, multiple solvent exposures can cause the media to shift or bleed, and extensive exposure to the solvent may well be required to accomplish the adhesive removal.

APPLYING THE SOLVENT

Once it is certain that the solvent is safe to use on the paper and media, remove the adhesive with the solvent.

1.   Place the solvent on the adhesive.
2.   On the non-image area, use a crepe square or "rubber cement pick-up square". Slowly pull the square over the adhesive and off the edge of the paper, onto a blotter. Keep cleaning the adhesive off the crepe square, so that it is not reapplied to the paper.

INSECTS

Silverfish, cockroaches, book lice, moths, flies and wood-boring beetles are all threats to paper art. They inhabit warm, dark and damp places. They eat glue, sizing and pastes. Since they are active in the dark, they can cause extensive damage to art before the customer realizes that insects are inside the frame.

To avoid risk of infesting the frame shop with paper-destructive bugs, do not open a frame that appears to contain active insects. They may inhabit the workshop. Take the work outside to open the frame or take these works to an exterminator. Or, better yet, as a paper conservator to recommend a certified exterminator.

To avoid risk of infesting the frame shop with paper-destructive bugs, do not open a frame that appears to contain active insects. They may inhabit the work-shop. Take the work outside to open the frame.

MOLD & MILDEW

Mold and mildew are fungi that thrive on non-living organic matter, such as paper. Fungi are particularly active in damp, humid environments. And because paper absorbs moisture from the air, it is highly vulnerable.

Mold damages the art by growing across the image, creating unsightly stains. Also, the mold weakens the paper by destroying its cellulose fibers.

Most fungi appears as furry, circular patches on the art. It may begin as white, fluffy spots, but as it develops it becomes black or greenish.

Treating mold growth is a multi-fold problem. All chemicals used to treat mold are toxic. Many are suspected carcinogens (cancer-producing substances) and others are known carcinogens. Also, these chemicals will alter the paper's fibers.

In the case of thymol, it will cause the paper to yellow. Not only are the chemicals toxic, but so are the molds. The Scottish Society for Conservation and Restoration reports that "some fungi and microorganisms may produce substances that are toxic or carcinogenic. Some species of aspergillus, and especially flavus, produce highly carcinogenic metabolites – the alfatoxins."

Given the toxicity level of all of the substances and the potential damage that the chemicals can cause the art, it is best to passively treat fungi. Rather than fumigating the art, get rid of its appearance on the art by drying it out. Mold will stop growing when the relative humidity drops below 70 percent. The first thing to do with an infected work is isolate it so the spores cannot spread throughout the workshop and infect other works.

Wear gloves. Then, take the art out of the frame and let it dry out for several days. It's best for the relative humidity in this drying area to be around 50 percent and the temperature to be 70 degrees. A small, portable de-humidifier can help achieve low humidity if necessary.

After the art has thoroughly dried, vacuum off the mold with a small vacuum cleaner, which is available from conservation suppliers. Vacuum up the mold rather than brush it off to prevent the mold spores from becoming airborne, and to prevent smearing mold across the face of the art.

Most fungi appear as furry, circular patches on the art. It may begin as white, fluffy spots, but as it develops it becomes black or greenish.

Try to have as little contact with the fungi as possible. If it is necessary to brush off the mold or work with the piece while it has mold on it, wear a dust respirator. Thoroughly wash hands afterwards.

Unless it has been fumigated, the art will still be contaminated. The spores of the fungi will lay dormant on the backing board, waiting to strike again. However, the mold cannot grow unless the relative humidity exceeds 70 percent. Advise the customer that the art must be placed in a humidity-controlled environment. If the art is going into a room which has central air-conditioning or dehumidifiers, the customer should not have further problems with mold growth. However, if the air-conditioning is periodically turned off, and/or the relative humidity is allowed to rise, again.

If the work is valuable, if the mold is widespread or if many works are involved, seek the advice of a paper conservator or a certified exterminator. This is clearly a situation where it is best to place the art in the hands of experts. Be aware that, while fumigation kills current mold spores and gives the art a very brief immunity against future attacks, new mold will probably grow on it if it is returned to a humid environment.

FOXING

It is not known whether or not foxing is a type of fungi. Foxing spots do not look hairy like mold, but look like reddish-brown stains or freckles. Because the stains look rusty and do not aggressively attack the paper like fungi, it is thought that foxing may be caused by minerals, such as iron, in the paper. To prevent foxing, it is best to keep the art in a low-humidity environment. Unfortunately, the only treatment for foxing is bleaching, which must be done by a professional conservator.

If the work is valuable, if the mold is widespread or if many works are involved, seek the advice of a paper conservator or a certified exterminator.

CHAPTER 11

STORAGE OF ARTWORK

Conservators have found that much deterioration of art is due to improper storage. When artwork is to be stored, rather than framed and placed on the wall, it must be properly packaged and situated. Tossed under the bed or rolled in a poster tube in the basement, or shoved in the back of the closet or attic are perfect examples of how many works are damaged.

Ideally, all valuable art should be matted before being placed in storage. The mat package provides the art with a rigid, non-acidic protector. It will help prevent dents, bends, stains, wrinkles and tears.

Artwork should be stored flat and protected against dust, mold, mildew, insects, air pollutants, acids and all the other enemies of paper. It should not be stored in damp basements, hot attics or sun porches. Areas near radiators or any other source of heat or dampness also are inappropriate.

A temperature- and humidity-controlled environment is ideal. Inspect stored artwork periodically.

GIVING CUSTOMERS ADVICE

If it is known that a customer will be storing the art, offer to assist, either by encapsulating the work or providing a good means of storing it, i.e., polyester envelopes or a flat box.

Art purchased purely for investment purposes should be kept in a safe, cool, dark place until it is time for it to be resold.

Customers may have fragile books or flaking pastels that they would rather not hang. Often, customers have more art than hanging space, so they may have to store part of their collection.

Some firms have art that they wish to preserve, particularly for their historical, informational or reproduction value, yet they feel it is inappropriate to keep them on continuous display. Such items might include original maps, drawings, documents, architectural renderings, graphic designs and photographs.

ENCAPSULATION

Encapsulation is an ideal method of storing art, especially if the work has been previously deacidified. It offers full protection. The work is encased in inert Mylar sheeting, and, if properly sealed, the work lives in a permanent microclimate. The work can easily be taken from storage, handled and

inspected, and no harm will come to it. It works particularly well for double-sided art, since both sides are visible.

However, if an acidic work has *not* been deacidified, encapsulation will not prevent the art from "self-destructing". In such cases, this method should be used only temporarily until the work can be treated. Do not use encapsulation with art that has loose media, such as charcoals, pastels and pencil drawings. See complete directions for encapsulation in chapter six.

TYPES OF STORAGE
1. Encapsulation see (Chapter 6)
2. Matboard Folders
3. Solander Boxes
4. Deep-sided Storage Box
5. Covered window mat

MATBOARD WITH WRAPPED FACE COVER

Art that has a design on only one side can be stored between a sheet of Mylar and sheet of rag matboard.

1. Using 2- or 4-ply rag or conservation matboard, cut a piece that is larger than the art.
2. Cut a piece of Mylar that is ½" larger, on all sides, than the matboard.
3. Crease the Mylar so it forms a rectangle that is about the same size as the matboard. Try not to make the corners too tight. Some air should circulate through the matting.
4. Hinge the art to the matboard.
5. Set the folded Mylar edges over the mat and tape onto the backside with double-sided tape.

Solander Box

Unframed art may be stored in special acid-free print boxes with hinged front panels which can be purchased from conservation suppliers. These storage units are often called solander boxes, named after 18th century Swedish botanist Daniel C. Solander.

Some say that he built the airtight boxes for his butterfly collections. The boxes are made in such a way that it is easy to store and remove paper art and delicate objects. The boxes are airtight with lids that open on one of the long sides. They may be made of sturdy, buffered acid-free board that has been lined either with a buffered paper or with a pH-neutral polyethylene.

A slip sheet of acid-free glassine, acid-free paper, or 5 mil Mylar should be used between art pieces in a stack. This protects the art from dirt and abrasion from other pieces in the stack. Loose-pigment works, such as charcoals, pastels and pencil drawings should be matted and "wrapped" before being stored. (see "Using a Cover")

The matted art should be stacked with the hinged sides facing forward, toward the hinged panel of the box. This consistency helps prevent picking up one mat package and part of the one underneath it, which could damage the support of that print or the print itself.

Making a Deep-Sided Storage Box

Storage boxes may be made from rag or acid-free boards and filler boards. A simple box can be made by scoring, then folding up the sides and taping the corners closed with pressure-sensitive tape. A lid is made by making another box slightly larger.

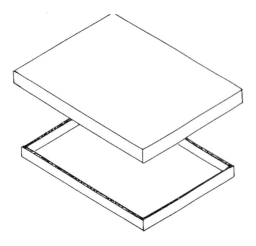

Using a Cover

Charcoals, pastels, graphites and fragile work need special protection while in storage. Since these works are powdery or flaky, their designs can be rubbed off or marred if they come into direct contact with a slip sheet.

First mat the art then add a fold-over cover to the window mat.

Cut a piece of matboard the same size as the matted art, put over the face of the mat and attach it to the mat along the long side with pressure-sensitive linen tape which will allow the spine to flex.

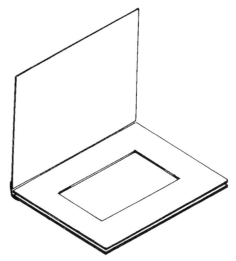

Storing Unmatted, Loose Art

Loose prints should be stored in shallow drawers or cabinets to eliminate scuffing and weight build-up. Store similar sizes together. Acidic works, especially news clippings, should be stored separately so the acid from these works does not migrate and contaminate the other works.

Use slipsheets such as rag, acid-free glassine, buffered papers or 5 mil. Mylar between the art. Loose media art, such as charcoals, pastels and graphites should not be stored loose, but matted and covered.

Storing Framed Art

Framed art should be stored vertically. Ideally, it is best to store the framed pieces in cabinets, separated by foam center board or felt-covered separators. For long-term storage, all wires and hanging devices should be removed from the frames to prevent damage to the other pieces.

CHAPTER 12

EXHIBIT & DISPLAY OF ARTWORK

Be sure to alert the customer to the limitations of glazing and framing. Explain the proper and improper places to hang it. Though displaying the finished framing is the customer's responsibility, if something goes wrong with the artwork, the framer will undoubtedly hear about it and will probably be asked to fix it.

Rather than give each customer a lecture on how to care for their art, the following tips could be listed in a brochure.

DISPLAYING AND CARING FOR FINE ART

Art on paper lives best in dark, low-humidity, temperate climates. For many years, art on paper was mainly kept in books or in albums. As parlor entertainment, these books were occasionally brought out and shown to friends and family. They were viewed much in the same way that we look at photo albums today. Since the prints were rarely exposed to light and atmospheric pollutants, they were conserved.

Today, art is part of our daily decor. We want to display it on our walls, so that we can constantly see it, enjoy it and show it off. Improper placement can jeopardize the art's condition and may eventually harm it.

The following tips should properly guide in caring for and displaying fine art or treasures.

• Expose art to the least amount of light possible. Direct sun can can cause many problems including bleaching pigments. Watch the pattern of sunlight where artwork hangs. Draw the curtains or blinds when the sun is strong or when going out for a long time. This will minimize damage from heat as well as from light.
Before the invention of clothes dryers, white clothes were put in the bright sunlight so that they would naturally bleach out and stay white. The same thing can happen to the art. Direct lighting causes colors to fade, change, darken or disappear. This detracts not only from the beauty of the work, but lessens its monetary value as well.

Artificial light should not be close to paper art, nor directed towards it. Keep spotlights, picture lights and track lights away from the face of the art.

• Use ultraviolet filtering sleeves over fluorescent lights. Ultraviolet rays emitted from fluorescent bulbs are as harmful as the sun's rays.

• Artwork should ideally be kept in an evenly-controlled environment approximately 70°F and 50 percent relative humidity. Air-conditioning is the best way to control the humidity, but do not hang the art directly across from the cold air flow of an air-conditioner.

• Never hang valuable art in high-humidity areas and areas that have extreme temperature fluctuations, such as a summer home or on a boat.

• Sometimes a print appears wrinkled inside of the frame. When there is excessive moisture in the air, the paper absorbs some of it and swells. This is natural. It is unrealistic to expect fine art to be absolutely flat in the frame. Art may appear slightly wrinkled in the summer and flat in the winter. The only way to avoid wrinkling is to keep the art in a humidity-controlled environment. If the wrinkling is severe and visually distracting, a framer should inspect the piece.

• A humid environment is a perfect breeding ground for insects, mold and foxing. To prevent humidity damage, do not hang prints on a wall that is damp or very cold. Fine art should not be placed in bathrooms, in damp basements or in unventilated rooms or closets.

• Do not hang fine art near radiators, opposite windows that have direct sunlight, or above a fireplace that is regularly used. Abrupt changing temperatures, heat, dust and ash from fires cause rapid and serious damage.

• Occasionally inspect the art. Check for mold or insect infestation. Both should be treated upon detection.

• Harmful conditions can develop even inside properly conserved and closed frames. Like all things of value, periodic inspection and maintenance is necessary. To prevent any long-term damage, have the artwork checked every five to 10 years by a professional framer.

Record of Condition Sheet

RECORD OF RECEIPT OF ARTWORK

Date _____   Examiner _____

Client _____   Storage Location _____

Address _____

_____   Brief Description _____

Phone _____

Value $ _____   Do we have a photograph of condition? _____

SIZE AND SHAPE OF ARTWORK
Height _____ x Width _____

MEDIUM
is characteristic of:
oil _____ watercolor _____ wax _____
acrylic _____ egg tempera _____
pastel _____ collage _____ pen & ink _____
children's tempera _____

CONDITION OF FRAME
no frame _____ good condition _____
dry & brittle _____ loose pieces _____

CONDITION OF STRETCHER BARS
OK _____ warped _____ infested _____ rotten _____

CONDITION OF SURFACE OR PAINT FILM
dirty _____ greasy _____ dry/brittle _____
blisters _____ flaking _____ scratched _____
buckling _____ cupping _____ crushed _____

SUPPORT
cotton canvas with ground _____ wood block _____
linen canvas with ground _____ sandpaper _____
cotton sheeting _____ other fabric _____
unprimed canvas _____ canvas panel _____
particle bd _____ metal _____ stone _____ tin _____
fiber bd _____ ivory _____ ceramic _____
rag paper _____ economy paper _____ mat bd _____
construction paper _____ other _____

CONDITION OF SUPPORT
dry & brittle _____ cracked _____ scratched _____
buckling _____ cupping _____ hole _____ tear _____
dent _____ pulls _____ missing pieces _____
other_____

VARNISH
No _____ Yes _____ crazed _____ peeling _____

GENERAL COMMENTS _____
_____
_____

APPENDIX B

CONSERVATOR RESOURCE

Restoration is an art. Conservators understand the chemistry, current methodology, materials and their potential problems. Professional restorers and conservators have invested years in building their expertise and instincts. They have the appropriate equipment at hand and can second guess the results of their techniques.

A competent conservator will use the greatest of caution with all restoration methods. They may be reached through a local museum, auction house, antique dealers, picture framers or the AIC.

The American Institute for the Conservation of Historic and Artistic Works (AIC) lists restorers by specialty in their annual directory. The Institute also operates the Conservation Services Referral System.

Professionals listed in the AIC's referral system specialize in such areas as: books and paper, objects, paintings, architecture, photographic materials, conservation science, wooden artifacts and textiles. There is no charge for using the AIC's referral system. The Northeast Document Conservation Center offers such services as conservation treatment, consulting and photographic copying.

Among the many services offered by conservators are: unmounting prints that have been glued down to a backing board, removing glue deposits from tapes, removing stains, treating mold and insect damage, repairing tears and creases, flattening buckled art, deacidifying works, and bleaching. The conservator carries out these procedures so as to maintain the original texture and characteristics of the art as much as possible.

Restorers' fees vary according to the problem. Some work on an hourly rate, while others base their fees on the type of treatment. Considering the time and expertise involved, it is certainly worth the costs for rare and valuable art. Be sure to discuss the maximum price and timing with the conservator. Conservation treatments are often long and complicated; be patient.

Resources:

The American Institute for the Conservation of Historic and Artistic Works (AIC)
Washington D.C. USA

The Institute of Paper Conservation
Worcestershire England

Manitoba Heritage Conservation Service
Winnipeg, Canada

Canadian Conservation Institute
Ottawa, Canada

Fine Arts Conservation Laboratory
Oberlin, Ohio USA

Northeast Document Center
Andover, Mass. USA

APPENDIX C

CONSERVATION SUPPLIES

ANW Crestwood
205 Chubb Ave.
Lyndhurst NJ 07071
papers & boards

Archival Products, LA
4129 Sepulveda Blvd.
Culver City, CA 90230
pastes, hinges, mending supplies

Archivart
7 Caesar Place
Moonachie, NJ 07074
general archival supplies

Archives USA
1101 King Street
Alexandria, VA 22314
general archival supplies

Archive Paper Company
2330 Midway Boulevard
P. O. Box 925
Broomfield, CO 80038-0925
mat & mount boards

Arlo Inc.
241 N. Clark Ave.
Los Altos, CA 94022
spacers

Bookkeeper Preservation Technologies
111 Thomson Park Drive
Cranberry Twp., PA 16066
deacidification materials

Conservation Resources International
8000-H Forbes Place
Springfield, VA 22151
general archival supplies

Crescent Cardboard Co.
100 West Willow Road
Wheeling, Il 60090-6587
mat & mount boards

Crescent Preservation Products
P. O. Box 285
Lenoxdale, MA 01242
museum boards

Cyro Industries
100 Enterprise Drive
P. O. Box 5055
Rockaway, NJ 07866
acrylic glazing

Denglas Technologies
8 Springdale Road
Cherry Hill, NJ 08003
glazing

Frame Tek Inc.
521 Market Street Suite D
Eugene, OR 97402
spacers

Gaylord Brothers
P. O. Box 4901
Syracuse NY 13221-4901
general archival supplies

Hollinger Corporation
P. O. Box 8360
Fredericksburg, VA 22404-8360
storage papers & boxes

Innerspace by Buckwalter
223 East King Street
Malvern, PA 19355-2517
spacers

International Paper
P. O. Box 1839
Statesville, NC 28687
mounting boards

Light Impressions Corporation
P. O. Box 940
Rochester, NY 14603
general archival supplies

Lineco Inc.
P. O. Box 2604
Holyoke, MA 01041
tapes, encapsulation envelopes

Metal Edge
2721 East 45th Street
Los Angeles, CA 90058
storage boxes

Nielsen & Bainbridge
40 Eisenhower Drive
Paramus, NJ 07652
mat & mounting boards

Plaskolite Inc.
P. O. Box 1497
Columbus, OH 43216-1497
acrylic glazing

Rising Paper
295 Park Street
Housatonic, MA 01236
mat & mount boards

Sandel Glass
110 W. Pontiac Way
P. O. Box 1107
Clovis, CA 93613
glazing

Vicki Schober Co.
2363 N. Mayfair Road
Milwaukee, WI 53226-1502
papers & boards

Seal Products Inc.
550 Spring Street
Naugatuck, CT 06770-9985
mounting tissue

Strathmore Paper
39 S. Broad Street
Westfield, MA 01085
artists papers

TALAS
568 Broadway
New York, NY 10012
general archival supplies

Tru Vue Inc.
1315 N. North Branch Street
Chicago, IL 60622-2413
glazing, matboards

University Products, Inc.
517 Main Street
P. O. Box 101
Holyoke, MA 01041-0101
general archival supplies

Wei T'o Associates Inc.
21750 Main Street Unit 27
Matteson, IL 60443-3702
deacidification materials

Zuel Co.
840 Hampden Ave.
St. Paul, MN 55114
glazing

BIBLIOGRAPHY

American Institute for Conservation of Historic and Artistic Works, The Book and Paper Group. *The Paper Conservation Catalog.* 5th ed., Washington, D.C.: AIC, BPG, 1988.

American Paper Institute, Inc. *The Dictionary of Paper.* Philadelphia: The Winchell Company, 1980.

Bachmann, Konstanze, ed. *Conservation Conserns: A Guide for Collectors and Curators.* Washington, D.C.: Smithsonian Institution Press, 1992.

Boris, Norman. "Alpha Cellulose: The Basis of All Permanent Papers". Picture Framing Magazine, August, 1993: 48-51.

Borowski, Elena. *The Cleaning of Prints, Drawings, and Manuscripts: Dry Methods.* Washington, D.C.: Smithsonian Institution Press, 1977.

Buchsbaum, Ann. *Practical Guide to Print Collecting.* New York: Van Nostrand Reinhold Company, 1975.

Clapp, Ann F. *Curatorial Care of Works of Art on Paper.* New York: Nick Lyons Books, 1987.

Clydesdale, Amanda. *Chemicals in Conservation: A Guide to Possible Hazards and Safe Use.* Scottish Society for Conservation Restoration, 1982.

Dawson, John. *The Complete Guide to Prints and Printmaking.* Quill Publishing, 1981.

Dolloff, Francis W. and Roy L. Perkinson. *How to Care for Works of Art on Paper.* 4th ed. Boston: Museum of Fine Arts, Boston, Mass., 1974.

Frederick, Paul. *The Framer's Book of Materials and Techniques.* St. Louis: Commerce Publishing Company, 1990.

Hauser, Robert. *Paper: Its History and Conservation.* Rising Paper Company, 1980.

Hunter, Dard. *Papermaking: The History and Technique of an Ancient Craft.* New York: Alfred P. Knopf, 1947.

Johnson, Arthur W. *The Practical Guide to Book Repair and Conservation.* London: Thames and Hudson Ltd., 1988.

Keefe, Jr., Laurence E. and Inch, Dennis. *The Life of a Photograph.* Stoneham, Mass.: Butterworth Publishers, 1984.

King, Louise. "To Giclée or Not to Giclée?" DECOR Magazine, February, 1997: 49-58.

Lamb, Allan R. *Framing Photography, Volume 6 of the Library of Professional Picture Framing.* Akron, OH: Columba Publishing, 1996.

Library of Congress. *Newsprint and Its Preservation.* National Preservation Program Publication, No. 5, Nov., 1981.

Library of Congress, *Papermaking Art and Craft,* 1968.

McGraw Hill Encyclopedia of Science and Technology., New York: McGraw Hill, 1995.

Mayer, Ralph. *The Artist's Handbook of Materials and Techniques.* New York: Viking Press, 1970.

Morrow, Carolyn Clark and Dyal, Carole. *Conservation Treatment Procedures.* Libraries Unlimited, Inc., 1986.

Murray, Peter and Linda. *The Penguin Dictionary of Art & Artists.* London: Penguin Books, 1983.

O'Neill, David. "The Giclée Way". DECOR Magazine, February, 1997: 61-64.

Parker, William P. *Glazing: A Practical Guide for Art Dealers and Picture Framers.* Akron, OH: Columba Publishing, 1991.

Pearlstein, E.J., Cabelli, D., King, A., and Indictor, N., "Effects of Eraser Treatment on Paper", Journal of the American Institute for Conservation, American Institute for Conservation of Historic and Artistic Works, Vol. 22, No. 1, Fall 1982.

Petherbridge, Guy. *Conservation of Library and Archive Materials and the Graphic Arts.* Stoneham, Mass.: Butterworth Publishers, 1987.

Phibbs, Hugh. "Preservation Hinging", Picture Framing Magazine, February, 1994: S4 - S24.

Pierce, Don. *Handle With Care: The Conservation And Matting of Art on Paper.* Crescent Cardboard Co., 1987.

Plenderleith, H. J. and Werner, A.E.A. *The Conservation of Antiquities and Works of Art.* Oxford University Press, 1988.

Professional Picture Framers Association. *PPFA Guild Guidelines for Framing Works of Art on Paper.* 1985.

Rempel, Siegfried. *The Care of Photographs.* New York: Nick Lyons Books, 1987.

Rosen, Randy. *Prints: The Facts and Fun of Collecting.* E.P. Dutton, 1978.

Shapiro, Cecile and Mason, Lauris. *Fine Prints: Collecting, Buying, and Selling.* New York: Harper & Row, 1976.

Shelley, Marjorie. *The Care and Handling of Art Objects: Practices in the Metropolitan Museum of Art.* 3d printing. New York: Metropolitan Museum of Art.

Skeist, Irving, ed. *Handbook of Adhesives.* 3d ed. New York: Van Nostrand Reinhold, 1990.

Smith, Merrily A. *Matting and Hinging of Works of Art on Paper.* The Consultant Press, 1986.

Thompson, John M. A. *Manual of Curatorship: A Guide to Museum Practice.* Stoneham, Mass.: Butterworth Publishers, 1984.

Turner, Sylvie. *Which Paper: A Guide to Choosing and Using Fine Papers for Artists, Craftspeople, and Designers.* New York: Lyons & Burford, 1994.

Warner, Glen. *Building a Print Collection.* New York: Van Nostrand Reinhold Company, 1981.

Zigrosser, Carl, and Gaehde, Christa M. *A Guide to the Collecting and Care of Original Prints.* Crown Publishers, Inc., 1975.

INDEX

A

acetone 36
acid-free 11, 24, 28, 32
acrylic adhesive 28
acrylic glazing 37
acrylic paints and mediums 38, 39, 59
adhesives 32, 34-36, 60
    for hinging 12, 32, 52, 74
    for repairs 76-78
    removal 27, 34, 36, 82, 84
adhesive release 36
advising customers 7-9, 36, 87-89
air bulbs 40, 72, 80, 82
air-conditioning 26, 85, 89
air pollution 22, 26
alkaline, alkalinity 10, 11, 24, 30-32, 55, 56, 70
alpha-cellulose 11, 30-31
alum 11, 12, 15-17, 31
animal skins 12, 14, 34, 62-63
animation cels 64
anti-reflective glass 37
antique papers 64, 68
Artsavers® 34, 42
Artsorb® 22
ATG® 35, 45, 48, 60, 66

B

backing board 11, 26-27, 32, 52-54
bark paintings 34, 64-65
barrier papers 32
blotter paper, blotting 11, 19, 40
bone folder 40
brushes 23, 40, 50
buffering 11, 17, 24, 26, 31, 32, 71
bumper pads 61

C

calcium carbonate 11, 17, 24, 26, 31, 32, 34, 40
canned air 40, 72
cast paper 54, 65
cellulose 11-13, 16, 22-25
cellophane tape 36, 82
chalk pastels 69

Cibachrome® photographs 72
cleaning surface dirt 40, 57, 77, 79-81
cockling 11, 22, 28, 70, 74
collages 21,66
computer-generated prints 66
conservators 91
conservation supplies 29-40, 92,
corner pockets 34, 42, 43, 62, 64
corrugated cardboard 27, 32, 59
crepe square 40, 84
currency 73

D

deacidification 11, 40, 55-57, 65
deckle 16-18
dehumidifiers 85
dimensional collage 66
disclaimer 8, 10
displaying art 7, 88, 89
document repair tape 35
double-sided mat 46, 48, 64, 73
dry cleaning pads 40, 80
dry mounting photographs 71
dust covers 11, 35, 59

E

edge strip supports 44
encapsulation 40, 42, 46, 47, 64, 72, 86
ethyl alcohol 40, 50
extra strength hinge 54

F

Filmoplast® 34, 72
filler board 27, 32, 59
fitting 59-60
flanges 42
flattening of prints 75, 91
float hinge 54, 64
float mounting 34, 52
fluorescent light 25, 89
foam center board 32, 48, 59, 66, 88
Fourdrinier machine 16, 18, 20
foxing 11, 21, 22, 86, 89
Framers Tape II 35
French mats 39
fumigating art 85

G

giclée 36, 66, 67
glazing 28, 36, 59
    acrylic 37, 52
    anti-reflective 36, 59
    glass 28, 36, 37
    non-glare 36-37
    optically coated 37
    spacing from art 37, 40, 69, 74
    styrene 37
    UV-filtering 25, 36, 37
    white, water white 36
gloves 40
gummed linen paper tape 34, 62, 70, 72

H

hanging hardware 61, 88
heat 7, 8, 22, 24, 26, 89
heat-set tapes 34, 78
hinges 49-54
    attaching 52
    drying 52, 53
    extra strength hinge 54
    float hinge 24, 64
    making 50
    T-hinge 47, 52
    V-hinge 53
    wet-cutting 50
    Z-hinge 53
Hollander beater 16
humidity 7, 8, 21, 22, 23, 84, 86, 88-89

I

Ilfochrome Classics® 72
inherent flaws 9, 26
insects 23, 84
Insta-Hinge® 34
Iris® prints 36, 66, 67

J

Japanese hinge removal 82
Japanese papers 19, 33, 34, 41, 49